U0111784

大展好書　好書大展
品嘗好書　冠群可期

大展好書　好書大展
品嘗好書　冠群可期

少林傳統功夫漢英對照系列　⑩

Shaolin Traditional Kungfu Series Books　⑩

　炮　拳

Cannon Boxing

耿　軍　著

Written by Geng Jun

大展出版社有限公司

作者簡介

耿軍（法號釋德君），1968 年 11 月出生於河南省孟州市，係少林寺三十一世皈依弟子。中國武術七段、全國十佳武術教練員、中國少林武術研究會副秘書長、焦作市政協十屆常委、濟南軍區特警部隊特邀武功總教練、洛陽師範學院客座教授、英才教育集團董事長。1989 年創辦孟州少林武術院、2001 年創辦英才雙語學校。先後獲得河南省優秀青年新聞人物、全國優秀武術教育家等榮譽稱號。

1983 年拜在少林寺住持素喜法師和著名武僧素法大師門下學藝，成爲大師的關門弟子，後經素法大師引薦，又隨螳螂拳一代宗師李占元、金剛力功于憲華等大師學藝。在中國鄭州國際少林武術節、全國武林精英大賽、全國武術演武大會等比賽中 6 次獲得少林武術冠軍；在中華傳統武術精粹大賽中獲得了象徵少林武術最高榮譽的「達摩杯」一座。他主講示範的 36 集《少林傳統功夫》教學片已由人民體育音像出版社出版發行。他曾多次率團出訪海外，在國際武術界享有較高聲譽。

炮拳

　　他創辦的孟州少林武術院，現已發展成爲豫北地區最大的以學習文化爲主、以武術爲辦學特色的封閉式、寄宿制學校，是中國十大武術教育基地之一。

Brief Introduction to the Author

作
者
簡
介

Geng Jun（also named Shidejun in Buddhism）, born in Mengzhou City of Henan Province, November 1968, is a Bud –dhist disciple of the 31st generation, the 7th section of Chinese Wu shu, national "Shijia" Wu shu coach, Vice Secretary General of China Shaolin Wu shu Research Society, standing committee member of 10th Political Consultative Conference of Jiaozuo City, invited General Kungfu Coach of special police of Jinan Military District, visiting professor of Luoyang Normal University, and Board Chairman of Yingcai Education Group. In 1989, he estab –lished Mengzhou Shaolin Wu shu Institute; in 2001, he estab –lished Yingcai Bilingual School · He has been successively awarded honorable titles of "Excellent Youth News Celebrity of Henan Province" "State Excellent Wu shu Educationalist" etc.

In 1983, he learned Wu shu from Suxi Rabbi, the Abbot of Shaolin Temple, and Grandmaster Sufa, a famous Wu shu monk, and became the last disciple of the

Grandmaster. Then recom-mended by Grandmaster Sufa, he learned Wu shu from masters such as Li Zhanyuan, great master of mantis boxing, and Yu Xianhua who specializes in Jingangli gong. He won the Shaolin Wu shu champion for 6 times in China Zhengzhou International Wu shu Festival, National Competition of Wu lin Elites, National Wu shu Performance Conference, etc. and one "Damo Trophy" that symbolizes the highest honor of Shaolin Wu shu in Chinese Traditional Wu shu Succinct Competition. 36 volumes teaching VCD of Shaolin Traditional Wu shu has been published and is-sued by People´s Sports Audio Visual Publishing House. He has led delegations to visit overseas for many times, enjoying high reputation in the martial art circle of the world.

Mengzhou Shaolin Wu shu Institute, established by him, has developed into the largest enclosed type boarding school of Yubei (north of Henan Province) area, which takes knowledge as primary and Wu shu as distinctiveness, also one of China´s top ten Wu shu education bases.

序　言

中華武術源遠流長，門類繁多。

少林武術源自嵩山少林寺，因寺齊名，是我國拳系中著名的流派之一。少林寺自北魏太和十九年建寺以來，已有一千五百多年的歷史。而少林武術也決不是哪一人哪一僧所獨創，它是歷代僧俗歷經漫長的生活歷程，根據生活所需逐步豐富完善而成。

據少林寺志記載許多少林僧人在出家之前就精通武術或慕少林之名而來或迫於生計或看破紅塵等諸多原因削髮爲僧投奔少林，少林寺歷來倡武，並經常派武僧下山，雲遊四方尋師學藝。還請武林高手到寺，如宋朝的福居禪師曾邀集十八家武林名家到寺切磋技藝，推動了少林武術的發展，使少林武術得諸家之長。

本書作者自幼習武，師承素喜、素法和螳螂拳李占元等多位名家，當年如饑似渴在少林寺研習功夫，曾多次在國內外大賽中獲獎。創辦的孟州少林武術院亦是全國著名的武術院校之一，他示範主講的 36 集《少林傳統功夫》教學 VCD 已由人民體育音像出版社發行。

本套叢書的三十多個少林傳統套路和實戰技法是少

林武術的主要內容，部分還是作者獨到心得，很值得一讀，該書還採用漢英文對照，使外國愛好者無語言障礙，爲少林武術走向世界做出了自己的貢獻，亦是可喜可賀之事。

　　　　　　　　　　　　　　　張耀庭題
　　　　　　　　　　　　　　　甲申秋月

Preface

Chinese Wushu is originated from ancient time and has a long history, it has various styles.

Shaolin Wushu named from the Shaolin Temple of Songshan Mountain, it is one of the famous styles in the Chinese boxing genre. Shaolin temple has more than 1500 years of history since its establishment in the 19th year of North Wei Taihe Dynasty. No one genre of Shaolin Wushu is created solely by any person or monk, but completed gradually by Buddhist monks and common people from generation to generation through long–lasting living course according to the requirements of life. As recording of Record of Shaolin Temple, many Shaolin Buddhist monks had already got a mastery of Wushu before they became a Buddhist monk, they came to Shaolin for tonsure to be a Buddhist monk due to many reasons such as admiring for the name of Shaolin, or by force of life or seeing through thevanity of life. The Shaolin Temple always promotes Wushu and frequently appoints Wushu Buddhist monks to go down the mountain to roam around for searching masters and learning Wushu from them. It also invites

Wushu experts to come to the temple, such as Buddhist monk Fuju of Song Dynasty, it once invited Wushu famous exports of 18 schools to come to the temple to make skill interchange, which promoted the development of Shaolin Wushu and made it absorb advantages of all other schools.

The author learned from many famous exports such as Suxi, Sufa and Li Zhanyuan of Mantis Boxing, he studied Chinese boxing eagerly in Shaolin Temple, and got lots of awards both at home and abroad, he also set up the Mengzhou Shaolin Wushu Institute, which is one of the most famous Wushu institutes around China. He makes demonstration and teaching in the 36 volumes teaching VCD of Shaolin Traditional Wushu, which have been published by Peoples sports Audio Visual publishing house.

There are more than 30 traditional Shaolin routines and practical techniques in this series of books, which are the main content of Shaolin Wushu, and part of which is the original things learned by the author, it is worthy of reading. The series books adopt Chinese and English versions, make foreign fans have no language barrier, and make contribution to Shaolin Wushu going to the world, which is delighting and congratulating thing.

Titled by Zhang Yaoting

目　錄
Contents

說　明 ……………………………………………… 13
Series Books Instructions

基本步型與基本手型 …………………………… 15
Basic stances and Basic hand forms

炮拳套路簡介 …………………………………… 25
Brief Introduction to the Routine Cannon Boxing

炮拳套路動作名稱 ……………………………… 26
Action Names of Routine Cannon Boxing

炮拳套路動作圖解 ……………………………… 29
Action Illustration of Routine Cannon Boxing

全套動作演示圖 ………………………………… 205
Demonstration of All the Action

炮

拳

説　明

　　（一）為了表述清楚，以圖像和文字對動作作了分解說明，練習時應力求連貫銜接。

　　（二）在文字說明中，除特別說明外，不論先寫或後寫身體的某一部分，各運動部位都要求協調活動、連貫銜接，切勿先後割裂。

　　（三）動作方向轉變以人體為準，標明前後左右。

　　（四）圖上的線條是表明這一動作到下一動作經過的線路及部位。左手、左腳及左轉均為虛線（┄┄►）；右手、右腳及右轉均為實線（──►）。

Instructions

(i) In order to explain clearly figures and words are used to describe the actions in multi steps. Try to keep coherent when exercising.

(ii) In the word instruction, unless special instruction, each action part of the body shall act harmoniously and join coherently no matter it is written first or last, please do not separate the actions.

(iii) The action direction shall be turned taking body as standard, which is marked with front, back, left or right.

(iv) The line in the figure shows the route and position from this action to the next action. The left hand, left foot and turn left are all showed in broken line ($\dashrightarrow$) ; the right hand, right foot and turn right are all showed in real line ($\longrightarrow$) .

基本步型與基本手型
Basic stances and Basic hand forms

圖 1

圖 2

圖 3

圖 4

圖 5

圖 6

圖 7

圖 8

圖 9

圖 10

圖 11

圖 12

基本步型與基本手型

圖 13

圖 14

圖 15

圖 16

圖 17

圖 18

圖 19

圖 20

圖 21

基本步型

少林武術中常見的步型有：弓步、馬步、仆步、虛步、歇步、坐盤步、丁步、併步、七星步、跪步、高虛步、翹腳步12種。

弓步：俗稱弓箭步。兩腿前後站立，兩腳相距本人腳長的4～5倍；前腿屈至大腿接近水平，腳尖微內扣不超過5°；後腿伸膝挺直，腳掌內扣45°。（圖1）

馬步：俗稱騎馬步。兩腳開立，相距本人腳長的3～3.5倍，兩腳尖朝前；屈膝下蹲大腿接近水平，膝蓋與兩腳尖上下成一條線。（圖2）

仆步：俗稱單叉，一腿屈膝全蹲，大腿貼緊小腿，膝微外展，另一腿直伸平仆接近地面，腳掌扣緊與小腿成90°夾角。（圖3）

虛步：又稱寒雞步。兩腳前後站立，前後相距本人腳長的2倍；重心移至後腿，後腿屈膝下蹲至大腿接近水平，腳掌外擺45°；前腿腳尖點地，兩膝相距10公分。（圖4）

歇步：兩腿左右交叉，靠近全蹲；前腳全腳掌著地，腳尖外展，後腳腳前掌著地，臀部微坐於後腿小腿上。（圖5）

坐盤步：在歇步的形狀下，坐於地上，後腿的大小腿外側和腳背均著地。（圖6）

基本步型與基本手型

　　丁步：兩腿併立，屈膝下蹲，大腿接近水平，一腳尖點地靠近另一腳內側腳窩處。（圖 7）

　　併步：兩腿併立，屈膝下蹲，大腿接近水平。（圖 8）

　　七星步：七星步是少林七星拳和大洪拳中獨有的步型。一腳內側腳窩內扣於另一腳腳尖，兩腿屈膝下蹲，接近水平。（圖 9）

　　跪步：又稱小蹬山步。兩腳前後站立，相距本人腳長的 2.5 倍，前腿屈膝下蹲，後腿下跪，接近地面，後腳腳跟離地。（圖 10）

　　高虛步：又稱高點步。兩腳前後站立，重心後移，後腿腳尖外擺 45°，前腿腳尖點地，兩腳尖相距一腳距離。（圖 11）

　　翹腳步：在七星螳螂拳中又稱七星步，兩腿前後站立，相距本人腳長的 1.5 倍，後腳尖外擺 45°，屈膝下蹲，前腿直伸，腳跟著地，腳尖微內扣。（圖 12）

基本手型

少林武術中常見的手型有拳、掌、鉤 3 種。

拳：

分為平拳和透心拳。

平拳：平拳是武術中較普遍的一種拳型，又稱方拳。四指屈向手心握緊，拇指橫屈扣緊食指。（圖

13）

透心拳：此拳主要用於打擊心窩處，故名。四指併攏捲握，中指突出拳面，拇指扣緊抵壓中指梢節處。（圖 14）

掌：

分為柳葉掌、八字掌、虎爪掌、鷹爪掌、鉗指掌。

柳葉掌：四指併立，拇指內扣。（圖 15）

八字掌：四指併立，拇指張開。（圖 16）

虎爪掌：五指分開，彎曲如鉤，形同虎爪。（圖 17）

鷹爪掌：又稱鎖喉手，拇指內扣，小指和無名指彎曲扣於掌心處，食指和中指分開內扣。（圖 18）

鉗指掌：五指分開，掌心內含。（圖 19）

鉤：

分為鉤手和螳螂鉤。

鉤手：屈腕，五指自然內合，指尖相攏。此鉤使用較廣，武術中提到的鉤均為此鉤。（圖 20）

螳螂鉤：又稱螳螂爪，屈腕成腕部上凸，無名指、小指屈指內握，食指、中指內扣，拇指梢端按貼於食指中節。（圖 21）

Basic stances

基
本
步
型
與
基
本
手
型

Usual stances in Shaolin Wushu are: bow stance, horse stance, crouch stance, empty stance, rest stance, cross – legged sitting, T – stance, feet – together stance, seven – star stance, kneel stance, high empty stance, and toes – raising stance, these twelve kinds.

Bow stance: commonly named bow – and – arrow stance. Two feet stand in tandem, the distance between two feet is about four or five times of length of one´s foot; the front leg bends to the extent of the thigh nearly horizontal with toes slightly turned inward by less than 5°; the back leg stretches straight with the sole turned inward by 45°. (Figure 1)

Horse stance: commonly named riding step. two feet stand apart, the distance between two feet is 3~3.5 times of length of one´s foot, with tiptoes turned forward; bend knees to squat downward, with thighs nearly horizontal, knees and two tiptoes in line. (Figure 2)

Crouch stance: commonly named single split. Bend the knee of one leg and squat entirely with thigh very close to lower leg and knee outspread slightly; straighten the other leg and crouch horizontally close to floor, keep the sole turned inward and forming an included angle of 90° with lower leg. (Figure 3)

Empty stance: also named cold – chicken stance. Two feet stand in tandem, the distance between two feet is 2 times of length of one´s foot; transfer the barycenter to back leg, bend the knee of the back leg and squat downward to the extent of the thigh nearly horizontal, with the sole turned outward by 45°; keep the tiptoe of front leg on the ground, with distance between two knees of 10cm. (Figure 4)

Rest stance: cross the two legs at left and right, keep them close and entirely squat; keep the whole sole of the front foot on the ground with tiptoes turned outward, the front sole of the back foot on the ground, and buttocks slightly seated on the lower leg of the back leg. (Figure 5)

Cross – legged sitting: in the posture of rest stance, sit on the ground, with the outer sides of the thigh and lower leg of the back leg and instep on the ground. (Figure 6)

T – stance: two legs stand with feet together, bend knees and squat to the extent of the thighs nearly horizontal, with one tiptoe on the ground and close to inner side of the fossa of the other foot. (Figure 7)

Feet – together stance: two legs stand with feet together, bend knees and squat to the extent of the thigh nearly horizontal. (Figure 8)

Seven – star stance: Seven – star step is a unique step form in Shaolin Seven – star Boxing and Major Flood Boxing. Keep the inner side of the fossa of one foot turned inward onto tiptoe of the other foot, bend two knees and squat nearly horizontal. (Figure 9)

Kneel stance: also named small mountaineering stance. Two feet stand in tandem, the distance between two feet is 2.5

times of length of one´s foot, bend knee of the front leg and squat, kneel the back leg close to the floor, with the heel of back foot off the floor. (Figure 10)

High empty stance: also named high point stance. Two feet stand in tandem. Transfer the barycenter backward, turn the tiptoe of the back leg outward by 45°, with tiptoe of front leg on the ground, and the distance between two tiptoes is length of one foot. (Figure 11)

Toes –raising stance: also named seven –star stance in Seven–star Mantis Boxing. Two legs stand in tandem, and the distance between two legs is 1.5 times of length of one´s foot. Keep the tiptoe of back leg turned outward by 45°, bend knees and squat, straighten the front leg with heel on the ground and tiptoe turned inward slightly. (Figure 12)

Basic hand forms

Usual hand forms in Shaolin Wushu are: fist, palm and hook, these three kinds.

Fist: classified into straight fist and heart–penetrating fist.

Flat fist: a rather common fist form in Wushu, also named square fist. Hold the four fingers tightly toward the palm, and horizontally bend the thumb to button up the fore finger. (Figure 13)

Heart –penetrating fist: mainly used for striking the heart part. Put four fingers together and coil –hold them, the middle finger thrusts out the striking surface of the fist, the thumb buttons up and presses the end and joint of the middle finger. (Figure 14)

Palm: classified into willow leaf palm, splay palm, tiger´s claw palm, eagle´s claw palm, fingers clamping palm.

Willow leaf palm: palm with four fingers up and thumb turned inward. (Figure 15)

Eight – shape palm: palm with four fingers up and thumb splay. (Figure 16)

Tiger´s claw palm: palm with five fingers apart, bent as hook and like tiger´s claw. (Figure 17)

Eagle´s claw palm: also named throat locking hand, with the thumb turned inward, the little finger and middle finger turned onto palm, fore finger and middle finger apart and turned inward. (Figure 18)

Fingers clamp palm: palm with five fingers apart and palm drawn in. (Figure 19)

Hook: classified into hook hand and mantis hook.

Hook hand: bend the wrist, five fingers drawn in naturally with fingertips together. This hook is used in wide range, the hook mentioned in Wushu refers to this. (Figure 20)

Mantis hook: also named mantis´ claw, bend wrist into wrist bulge upward, the ring finger and little finger bend to hold inward, with fore finger and fore middle finger turned inward and end of thumb pressed on the middle joint of the fore finger. (Figure 21)

炮拳套路簡介

Brief Introduction to the Routine Cannon Boxing

　　少林炮拳古稱炮捶，是少林寺秘不外傳的精華套路，有「諸拳之王」之稱。因出拳威猛如發炮，拳勢動作多以炮為名，故名炮拳，本套路由45動作組成，適合有一定少林拳基礎者演練。

　　Shaolin Cannon boxing, anciently named cannon pounding, is a secret essential routine, with the title of "King of boxing". It is named cannon boxing for its forceful and swift fist like cannon and most its actions are named after cannon. This routine consists of 45 movements. and it is suitable for the persons who has certain wushu base to perform or practise.

炮拳套路動作名稱
Action Names of Routine
Cannon Boxing

第一段　Section　One

1. 預備勢　Preparatory position
2. 撩手摘心捶　Heart–picking fist with hand uppercut
3. 轉身窩心捶　Heart–punching fist with body turn
4. 馬步沖天炮　Sky cannon in horse stance
5. 五花虎抱頭　Swing arms into tiger holds head
6. 轉身雲頂七星　Turn body and cloud top into
　　　　　　　　　seven–star
7. 轉身單鞭　Single whip with body turn
8. 五花虎抱頭　Swing arms into tiger holds head
9. 上步左斜形　Step forward into left diagonal
　　　　　　　posture
10. 勒手小束身　Rein hand to shrink body
11. 上步左斜形　Step forward into left diagonal
　　　　　　　posture
12. 劈腿右斜形　Leg split with right diagonal posture
13. 十字採腳　Slap cross foot
14. 轉身窩心捶　Heart–punching fist with body turn

15. 馬步沖天炮　Sky cannon in horse stance

第二段　Section　Two

16. 攔腰雙絕手　Grasp waist for double punches
17. 抬腿小提鞋　Raise the leg to lift small shoe
18. 落步右拐肘　Land step and bend right elbow
19. 轉身雙絕雙分腿　Double punches and double separations with body turn
20. 起身雙風貫耳　Raise to strike the opponent's ears with both fists
21. 起手迎面捶　Raise hand and strike face with hammer
22. 轉身雲頂七星　Turn body and cloud top into seven-star
23. 轉身單鞭　Single whip with body turn
24. 五花虎抱頭　Swing arms into tiger holds head
25. 搖身三臥枕　Sway body to rest on the pillow three times
26. 轉身窩心捶　Turn body to punch heart with hammer
27. 倒步沖天炮　Sky cannon with backward step

第三段　Section　Three

28. 轉身單叉　Single split with body turn

29. 起身拐肘　Rise body and bend elbow

30. 轉身雙絕雙分腿　Double punches and double separa−tions with body turn

31. 起身雙風貫耳　Rise body to strike the opponent´s ears with both fists

32. 劈腿左斜形　Splitting leg with left diagonal posture

33. 劈腿右斜形　Splitting leg with right diagonal posture

34. 恨腳海底炮　Stamping the foot for cannon at the bottom of sea

35. 上步兩捶　Step forward and punch twice

36. 叉步斜形　Diagonal posture in cross stance

37. 回身一捶　Turn round and punch

第四段　Section Four

38. 轉身雙絕雙分腿　Double punches and double separations with body turn

39. 起身雙風貫耳　Rise body to strike the opponent´s ears with both fists

40. 轉身躍步單叉　Turn body and jump into single split

41. 起身沖天炮　Sky cannon with body rise

42. 束身下劈腿　Shrink body and hack down

43. 起身五指朝鳳   Fingers toward the phoenix with body rise

44. 轉身雲頂七星   Turn body and cloud top into seven stars

45. 馬步單鞭   Single whip in horse stance

46. 五花坐山   Swing arms with horse stance

47. 收勢   Closing form

炮拳套路動作名稱

炮拳套路動作圖解

Action Illustrtion of Routine Cannon Boxing

圖1

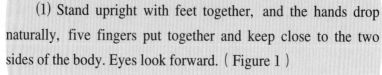

第一段　Section One

1.預備勢　Preparatory position

(1) 兩腳併立；兩手自然下垂，五指併攏，貼於體側；目視前方。（圖1）

(1) Stand upright with feet together, and the hands drop naturally, five fingers put together and keep close to the two sides of the body. Eyes look forward.〔Figure 1〕

炮拳套路動作圖解

圖 2

(2)左腳向左側橫跨一步，腳與肩同寬；同時，兩手變拳上提，抱於兩腰間；目視左方。（圖 2）

要點：頭正頸直。挺胸收腹，抱拳迅速。

(2) The left foot strides a step to the left side, with the feet at shoulder-width apart. Two hands change into fists and lift upward to hold on the waist. Eyes look leftward.〔Figure 2〕

Key points: head and neck upright. Lift the chest and draw in the abdomen, hold fists quickly.

圖 3

2. 撩手摘心捶
Heart-picking fist with hand uppercut

（1）接上勢。右拳不動；左拳變掌前伸，並向左方平畫，掌心向外，高與肩平；目視左方。（圖 3）

(1) Follow the above posture, keep the right fist st–ationary, change the left fist into palm, stretch the palm forward and horizontally swing it leftward, with the palm outward, at the shoulders height. Eyes look leftward.（Figure 3）

圖 4

(2) 上動不停。左腳尖外擺，身體左轉 90°，右腳向前搓地，提膝成獨立勢；同時，左掌外撩，隨即抓握變拳，左臂屈肘收於胸前；右拳向上、向外屈肘挑臂，拳心向裏，拳面向上，高與頜平；左拳拳心向下貼於右肘窩處；目視右拳。（圖 4）

(2) Keep the above action, the left tiptoe turns outward, and the body turns 90° to the left. The right foot rubs the ground forward, then lift the left knee into single –leg stance. At the same time, the left palm thrusts outward, then grabs into fist, the left elbow bends to draw back the left arm in front of the chest; bend the right elbow to raise the arm upward and outward, with the fist–palm inward, the fist–plane up, at chin height. Press the left fist to the right cubital fossa, with the palm side downward. Eyes look at the right fist.（Figure 4）

炮拳

圖5

(3)上動不停。右腳向右落步成馬步;同時,右拳裏旋,經胸前向右下方推按,拳面斜向下,置於右膝外側;目視右拳。(圖5、圖5附圖)

要點:轉身迅速,馬步與右拳同時完成,力達拳輪。

圖 5 附圖

(3) Keep the above action, the right foot lands rightward into horse stance. At the same time, rotate the right fist inward, push and press it right downward through the front of the chest, with the fist –plane down aslant, and place the right fist at the outer side of the right knee. Eyes look at the right fist. (Figure 5, Attached figure 5)

Key points: turn the body quickly, complete the actions of horse stance and the right fist simultaneously with the strength that shall reach the fist–wheel.

炮

拳

圖 6

3. 轉身窩心捶
Heart-punching fist with body turn

（1）接上勢。身體略向左轉；同時，左拳變掌，由外向裏屈肘按掌，掌心向下，掌指向前；右拳抱於腰間，拳心向上；目視左掌。（圖6）

(1) Follow the above posture, the body slightly turns to the left. At the same time, the left fist changes into palm, the left elbow bends to press the palm from outward to inward, with the palm down and the fingers forward; hold the right fist on the waist, with the fist-palm up. Eyes look at the left palm.（Figure 6）

圖 7

(2) 上動不停。身體左轉 90°，重心前移成左弓
步；右拳拳心向上，向前沖拳，與腰同高；左掌屈肘
回收，置於右臂肘窩處，掌心向下；目視右拳。（圖
7）

(2) Keep the above action, turn the body 90° to the left, shift
the barycenter forward into left bow stance. Punch the right fist
forward, with the fist–palm up, at the waists height. Bend the left
elbow to draw back the left palm, and place the left palm at the
right cubital fossa, with the palm down. Eyes look at the right
fist.（Figure 7）

炮

拳

圖 8

(3) 上動不停。身體右轉 90°，重心右移成馬步；
同時，右拳收抱於腰間，拳心向上；左掌向左下方橫
掌推出，置於左膝外側，掌心斜向下，掌指向前；目
視左掌。（圖 8）

要點：整個動作要連貫迅速，協調一致。

Keep the above action, turn the body 90° to the right, and
shift the barycenter rightward into horse stance. At the same
time, draw back and hold the right fist on the waist, with the
fist－palm up; push the left horizontal palm left downward, and
place it at the outer side of the left knee, with the palm
downward aslant. Eyes look at the left palm.（Figure 8）

Key points: the whole action shall be coherent and quick,
harmonious and consistent.

炮拳套路動作圖解

圖 9

4. 馬步沖天炮　Sky cannon in horse stance

（1）接上勢。身體左轉 90°，重心略向後移；同時，左掌變拳，兩拳同時向左後方掄臂擺拳，拳心均向下，高與胯平。（圖 9）

(1)Follow the above posture, turn the body 90° to the left, shift the barycenter backward slightly. At the same time, change the left palm into fist, and swing the two fists left backward simultaneously through brandishing the arms, with both the fist-palms down, at hip height.（Figure 9）

炮拳

圖 10

(2)上動不停。身體右轉 90°成馬步；同時，右拳經面前向右掄拳；左拳繼續向後、向上擺拳，兩臂呈水平，兩拳眼均向上；目視右拳。（圖 10、圖 10 附圖）

炮拳套路動作圖解

圖 10 附圖

(2) Keep the above action, turn the body 90° to the right into horse stance. At the same time, swing the right fist rightward through the front of faces; continuously swing the left fist backward and upward. Keep the two arms horizontal, with both the fist–holes up. Eyes look at the right fist. (Figure 10, Attached figure 10)

圖 11

（3）上動不停。身體略向右轉，重心略右移；同時，掄左臂向上、向前掄拳，拳心向裏，拳眼向上；右臂向下、向後擺拳，拳心向外，兩拳左前右後呈水平。（圖 11、圖 11 附圖）

炮
拳
套
路
動
作
圖
解

圖 11 附圖

(3) Keep the above action, turn the body to the right slightly, and shift the barycenter rightward slightly. At the same time, swing the left fist upward and forward by brandishing the left arm, with the fist–palm inward and the fist–hole up. Swing the right fist downward and backward, with the fist–palm outward. Keep the two fists horizontal at left forward and right backward. 〔 Figure 11, Attached figure 11 〕

炮
拳

圖 12

(4) 上動不停。右拳向前掄拳，與左拳同時收抱於
腰間，拳心向上；目視兩拳。（圖 12、圖 12 附圖）

炮
拳
套
路
動
作
圖
解

圖 12 附圖

(4) Keep the above action, brandish the right fist forward, draw back it and hold it with the left one on the waist simultaneously, with the fist-palms up. Eyes look at the two fists. ﹝ Figure 12, Attached figure 12 ﹞

圖 13

（5）上動不停。起身兩腿直立；兩拳經胸前向左上方沖拳，拳面向上，拳心向裏，右拳在裏高與頭平，左拳在外，略高於右拳；目視兩拳。（圖 13）

(5) Keep the above action, raise the body, with both the legs standing upright. Punch the two fists left upward through the front of the chest, with both fist-planes up and fist-palms inward. Keep the right fist inside at the head level, and the left one outside, slightly higher than the right fist. Eyes look at the two fists.〔Figure 13〕

炮拳套路動作圖解

圖 14

(6) 上動不停。身體下蹲成馬步；同時，兩臂屈肘回收於胸前，左拳落於左耳側，右拳落於左胸前，兩拳心均向右，拳面均向上；目視右方。（圖 14）

要點：轉身要迅速，兩腳蹬地，猛力向上抖肩沖拳，力達拳面。

(6) Keep the above action, the body squats into horse stance. At the same time, bend the two elbows to draw back the two arms in front of the chest, with the left fist falling at the left ear side and the right one falling in front of the left chest. Keep both the fist-palms rightward and the fist-planes up. Eyes look rightward.（Figure 14）

Key points: turn the body quickly, the feet kick the ground, snap the shoulders to punch the fists upward with sudden strength that shall reach the striking surfaces of the fists .

圖 15

5. 五花虎抱頭
Swing arms into tiger holds head

(1) 接上勢。身體略向右轉；同時，左臂伸直，隨身向左前方掄出，拳心向裏，拳眼向上；右臂向後、向上擺動，拳心向外，目視左拳。（圖 15、圖 15 附圖）

炮拳套路動作圖解

圖 15 附圖

(1) Follow the above posture, turn the body to the ri ght slightly. At the same time, straighten the left arm and swing it left forward with body turn, keep the fist–palm inward and the fist–hole upward; swing the right arm backward and upward, with the fist–palm outward. Eyes look at the left fist. (Figure 15, Attached figure 15)

炮
拳

圖 16

（2）上動不停。身體略向左轉，重心移至左腿，右
腳收於左腳內側，腳尖點地，身體下蹲成右丁步；同
時，左拳經腹前向左、向上擺架，置於頭左上方，拳
心斜向上；右拳向上、向裏屈臂盤肘，經面前下落於
左腰前，肘尖向前，拳眼向裏，拳心向下；目視右
方。（圖 16、圖16 附圖）

圖 16 附圖

(2) Keep the above action, turn the body to the left slightly, and shift the barycenter to the left leg. Draw the right foot at the inner side of the left one, with the tiptoe on ground, and squat into right T–stance. At the same time, swing and parry the left fist leftward and upward through the front of the abdomen, and place it above the left part of the head, with the fist–palm upward aslant. Bend the right arm to cross the elbows upward and inward, and the right fist fall in front of the left waist through the front of the faces, keep the elbow joint forward, the fist–hole inward and the fist–palm down. Eyes look rightward.
(Figure 16, Attached figure 16)

圖 17

6. 轉身雲頂七星
Turn body and cloud top into seven-star

（1）接上勢。身體起立右轉 180°，右腳提起，隨轉身向右邁一步；同時，兩拳變掌，右掌經胸前向外、向上雲托置於頭右側方，高與頭頂平；左掌置於頭頂上方，兩掌心均向上，掌指均向右；目視右掌。（圖 17）

（1）Follow the above posture, raise the body and turn it 180° to the right, the right foot lifts and strides a step rightward. At the same time, change the two fists into palms, cloud the right palm outward and upward through the front of the chest and place it at the right side of the head, at the head height; place the left palm above the head. Keep both the palms upward and the fingers rightward. Eyes look at the right palm.（Figure 17）

炮拳套路動作圖解

圖 18

(2) 上動不停。右腳尖外擺，身體右轉 90°；同時，兩掌經頭頂，左手在前，右手在後，自右向左雲托，隨即收抱於腰間，拳心向上；目視前方。（圖 18）

(2) Keep the above action, turn the right tiptoe out–ward, and turn the body 90° to the right. At the same time, swing the two palms through the head top from the right to the left, with the left right hand behind the left one, then draw back and hold them on the waist, with the fist–palms up. Eyes look forward. (Figure 18)

圖 19

　（3）上動不停。左腳向前上步成丁步；同時，右拳
向前平沖，拳心向下，高與肩平；左臂屈肘前撐，拳
面抵於右肘內側，拳心向下；目視右拳。（圖 19）

　　要點：雲頂動作與轉體要密切配合，協調完成，
纏頭幅度不宜太大。右沖拳與成丁步要一致。

　（3）Keep the above action, the left foot steps fo-rward into
T-stance. At the same time, horizontally punch the right fist
forward, with the fist-palm down, at the shoulders height; bend
the left elbow for forward support, keep the fist-plane close to
the inner side of the right elbow, with the fist-centre down. Eyes
look at the right fist.（Figure 19）

　　Key points: the action of clouding-top and the body turn
shall cooperate closely, and be completely harmoniously, with
not to large amplitude of twining the head. The right punch and
changing into T-stance shall be consist.

炮拳套路動作圖解

圖 20

7. 轉身單鞭　Single whip with body turn

（1）接上勢。身體左轉 90°，左腳向左橫跨一步成馬步；同時，兩拳內旋，屈肘合於胸前併齊，拳心向裏，高與肩平；目視兩拳。（圖 20）

(1) Follow the above posture, turn the body 90° to the left, and the left foot strides a step leftward into horse stance. At the same time, rotate the two fists inward, bend the elbows to combine the two fists in front of the chest and put them together, with the fist–palm inward, at the shoulders height. Eyes look at the two fists.（Figure 20）

炮
拳

圖 21

(2) 上動不停。兩拳分別向身體兩側平沖，拳心均
向下，拳眼均向前，高與肩平；目視左拳。（圖 21）

(2) Keep the above action, horizontally punch the two fists
to both sides of the body respectively, with both the fist-palms
downward and the fist-holes forward, at the shoulders height.
Eyes look at the left fist.（Figure 21）

炮拳套路動作圖解

圖 22

8. 五花虎抱頭
Swing arms into tiger holds head

（1）接上勢。身體略向右轉，重心稍上提；同時，左臂隨身向上、向前直臂掄擺拳於胸前，拳心向裏，拳眼向上；右臂向下、向後擺拳，拳眼向下，兩臂呈水平。（圖 22）

(1) Follow the above posture, turn the body to the right slightly, and raise the barycenter slightly. At the same time, brandish the left arm upward and forward with the arm straight to swing the fist in front of the chest with body turn, keep the fist−palm inward and the fist−hole up; swing the right fist downward and backward, with the fist−hole down. Keep the two arms horizontal.（Figure 22）

炮
拳

圖 23

(2) 上動不停。身體略向左轉，重心移至左腿；同時，右臂隨身向上、向前直臂擺拳，置於身體右前方，拳心向裏，拳眼向上；左臂向下、向後擺拳，拳眼向下，兩臂呈水平；目視右拳。（圖 23）

(2) Keep the above action, turn the body to the left slightly, and shift the barycenter to the left leg. At the same time, swing the right fist upward and forward with the right arm straight and body turn, and place it before the right of the body, with the fist−palm inward and fist−hole up; swing the left fist downward and backward, with the fist−hole down. Keep the two arms horizontal. Eyes look at the right fist.（Figure 23）

圖 24

（3）上動不停。身體略向右轉，重心移至右腿，左
腳收於右腳內側，腳尖點地成左丁步；同時，右臂隨
身向右、向上擺架拳於頭前上方，拳心向前，拳眼向
下；左臂隨身向前、向裏擺拳，屈臂盤肘，左拳落於
腹前，拳心向下，拳眼向裏；目視左方。（圖 24）

(3) Keep the above action, turn the body to the right slightly,
and shift the barycenter to the right leg. Draw back the left foot
to the inner side of the right one, with the tiptoe on ground into
left T-stance. At the same time, swing and parry the right fist
rightward and upward to the fore above the head with body turn,
keep the fist-palm forward and fist-hole down; swing the left
fist forward and inward with body turn, bend the arm to cross the
elbow, and the left fist falls in front of the abdomen, with the
fist-palm down and fist-hole inward. Eyes look leftward.
（Figure 24）

炮

拳

圖 25

9. 上步左斜形
Step forward into left diagonal posture

(1) 接上勢。左腳向左橫跨一步成馬步；同時，右拳下落，與左拳交叉抱於胸前，右拳在裏，左拳在外，兩拳心均向裏；目視兩拳。（圖 25）

(1) Follow the above posture, the left foot strides a step leftward into horse stance. At the same time, the right fist falls, cross it with the left one and hold them in front of the chest, with the right fist inside and the left one outside. Keep both the fist–palms inward. Eyes look at the two fists.〔Figure 25〕

炮拳套路動作圖解

圖 26

(2)上動不停。左腳尖外擺，身體左轉 90°，重心前移成左弓步；同時，左拳隨身向後撐拳，右拳向前撐拳，兩臂微屈，拳眼相對，兩拳心均向下，高與肩平；目視前方。（圖 26）

要點：轉身迅速，撐拳時要蹬腿、擰腰、催肩撐臂，力達前臂外緣。

(2) Keep the above action, turn the left tiptoe outward, turn the body 90° to the left, and shift the barycenter forward into left bow stance. At the same time, support the left fist backward with body turn, and support the right one forward. Bend the two arms slightly, with the fist–holes opposite and both the fist–palms down, at shoulders height. Eyes look forward. (Figure 26)

Key points: turn the body quickly; kick, twist the waist, move the shoulders and support the arms when supporting the fists, with the strength that shall reach the outer edge of the forearm.

圖 27

10. 勒手小束身　Rein hand to shrink body

(1) 接上勢。下身姿勢不變；兩拳變掌，左掌向前，臂微屈，置於右臂外側，與右掌交叉於胸前，右掌心向前，左掌心向右，掌指向上；目視前方。（圖27）

(1) Follow the above posture, keep the posture of the lower body. Change the two fists into palms with the left one forward, bend the left arm slightly and place the left palm at the outer side of the right arm to cross it with the right palm in front of the chest. Keep the right palm forward and the left one rightward, with the fingers up. Eyes look forward.（Figure 27）

炮拳套路動作圖解

圖 28

(2) 上動不停。重心移至右腿，左腳收回腳尖點地，身體後坐成左虛步；同時，兩掌翻腕變拳，屈肘收於胸前。左拳在前，高與肩平，右拳在後，略低於左拳，兩拳拳心均向裏，拳面均向上；目視前方。（圖 28）

要點：重心穩固，兩拳回拉要迅速有力。

(2) Keep the above action, shift the barycenter to the right leg, draw back the left foot with the tiptoe on ground, draw the body backward into left empty stance. At the same time, turn over the two wrists to change the two palms into fists, bend the elbows to draw back the fists in front of the chest. Keep the left fist before at the shoulders level, and the right one behind, slightly lower than the left one; both the fist-palms inward and fist-planes up. Eyes look forward.（Figure 28）

Key points: the barycenter shall be firm, and drawing back the two fists shall be quick and forceful.

圖 29

11. 上步左斜形
Step forward into left diagonal posture

(1) 接上勢。身體右轉 90°，左腳向左橫開一步成
馬步；同時，左拳下落，與右拳交叉抱於胸前，右拳
在裏，左拳在外。兩拳心均向裏；目視兩拳。（圖
29）

(1) Follow the above posture, the body turns 90° to the right,
the left foot strides a step leftward into horse stance. At the same
time, the left fist falls, cross the two fists and hold them in front
of the chest, keep the right fist inside and the left one outside,
with both the fist-palms inward. Eyes look at the two fists.
（Figure 29）

炮拳套路動作圖解

圖 30

(2) 上動不停。左腳尖外擺，身體左轉 90°，重心前移成左弓步；同時，左拳隨身向後撐拳，右拳向前撐拳，兩臂微屈，拳眼相對，兩拳心均向下，高與肩平；目視前方。（圖 30）

要點：同第 9 式。

(2) Keep the above action, turn the left tiptoe out-ward, and turn the body 90° to the left, shift the bary-center forward into left horse stance. At the same time, support the left fist backward with body turn, and support the right one forward. Bend the two arms slightly, with the fist-holes opposite and both the fist-palms down, at the shoulders height. Eyes look forward. （Figure 30）

Key points: the same as that of Posture 9.

圖 31

12. 劈腿右斜形
Leg split with right diagonal posture

（1）接上勢。左拳收於腰間，拳心向上；右拳向上、向後擺拳，置於右耳側，拳面向後，拳心向裏；目視前方。（圖31）

(1) Follow the above posture, draw back the left fist on the waist, with the fist–centre up; swing the right fist upward and backward, and place it at the right ear side, with the fist–plane backward and the fist–palm inward. Eyes look forward.（Figure 31）

圖 32

(2) 上動不停。重心前移至左腿，右腿抬起向前正踢腿；同時，右拳經右腿外側向下劈拳，落於身右側，拳心向裏，拳面向下；目視右腳。（圖 32）

(2) Keep the above action, move the barycenter to the left leg, and the right leg lifts to kick forward. At the same time, hack the right fist downward through the outer side of the right leg, then the right fist falls to the right side of the body, with the fist–palm inward and the fist–plane down. Eyes look at the right foot.（Figure 32）

炮
拳

圖 33

(3) 上動不停。身體左轉 90°，右腳向右落步成馬步；同時，兩拳從外向裏畫弧，交叉合抱於胸前，右拳在外，左拳在裏，兩拳心均向裏；目視兩拳。（圖33）

(3) Keep the above action, the body turns 90° to the left, and the right foot falls rightward into horse stance. At the same time, the two fists draw a curve from outward to inward, then cross and hold them in front of the chest. Keep the right fist outside and the left one inside, with both fist-palms inward. Eyes look at the two fists. ﹝ Figure 33 ﹞

圖 34

(4) 上動不停。右腳尖外擺，身體右轉 90°，重心前移成右弓步；同時，右拳隨身向後撐拳，左拳向前撐拳，兩臂微屈，拳眼相對，兩拳心均向下，高與肩平；目視前方。（圖 34）

要點：踢腿要高，右劈拳與踢腿要一致，力達拳輪。撐拳時要蹬腿擰腰，力達前臂外緣。

炮
拳

Figure 34

(4) Keep the above action, turn the right tiptoe out-ward, and turn the body 90° to the right, shift the bary-center forward into right bow stance. At the same time, support the right fist backward with body turn, and support the left one forward. Bend the two arms slightly, with the two fist-holes opposite and both the two fist-palms down, at the shoulders height. Eyes look forward. (Figure 34)

Key points: kick highly, hacking the right fist shall be consist with the kick, with the strength reaching the palm ring. When supporting the fists, kick the legs and twist the waists, with the strength reaching the outer edges of the forearms.

圖 35

13. 十字採腳　Slap cross foot

(1) 接上勢。重心移至右腿，左腿向上方踢腿，腳面繃直；同時，右拳變掌，從後向前拍擊左腳面；左拳抱於腰間，拳心向上；目視右掌（圖 35）

(1) Follow the above posture, shift the barycenter to the right leg. The left leg kicks upward, with the instep stretching straight. At the same time, the right fist changes into palm and slaps the left instep form backward to forward; hold the left fist on the waist with the fist–palm up. Eyes look at the right palm. (Figure 35)

圖 36

(2) 上動不停。左腳向下落步，右腿抬起向上踢腿；同時，右掌變拳，收抱於腰間，拳心向上；左拳變掌，向前拍擊右腳面；目視左掌。（圖 36）

(2) Keep the above action, the left foot falls, and the right leg lifts to kick upward. At the same time, change the right palm into fist, draw back and hold the right fist on the waist, with the fist–palm up; change the left fist into palm and slap the right instep forward with the left palm. Eyes look at the left palm.〔Figure 36〕

炮拳套路動作圖解

圖 37

(3) 上動不停。右腳向下落步，左腿抬起向上踢腿；同時，左掌變拳，收抱於腰間，拳心向上；右拳變掌，向前拍擊左腳面；目視右掌。（圖 37）

要點：踢腿過腰，擊響力點準確，聲音響亮，整個動作要迅速連貫。

(3) Keep the above action, the right foot falls, and the left leg lifts to kick upward. At the same time, change the left palm into fist, draw back and hold the left fist on the waist, with the fist–palm up; change the right fist into palm and slap the left instep forward with the right palm. Eyes look at the right palm. (Figure 37)

Key points: kick the leg to the height higher than the waist, with exact slap point and loud sound, and the whole action shall be quick and coherent.

圖 38

14. 轉身窩心捶
Heart-punching fist with body turn

（1）接上勢。身體左轉 90°，左腳向左方落步成馬步；同時，左拳變掌，由外向裏屈肘按掌，掌心向下；右掌變拳，抱於腰間，拳心向上；目視左方。（圖 38）

(1) Follow the above posture, the body turns 90° to the left, and the left foot falls leftward into horse stance. At the same time, change the left fist into palm, bend the left elbow and press the left palm from outward to inward, with the palm down; change the right palm into fist and hold the right fist on the waist, with the fist-palm up. Eyes look leftward. (Figure 38)

圖 39

(2) 上動不停。身體繼續左轉 90°，左腳尖外擺，重心前移成左弓步；同時，右拳向前沖拳，拳心向上，拳面向前；左臂屈肘，左掌收回置於右肘肘窩處，掌心向下；目視右拳。（圖 39）

(2) Keep the above action, the body continues to turn 90° to the left. Turn the left tiptoe outward, and shift the barycenter forward into left bow stance. At the same time, punch the right fist forward, with the fist–palm up and the fist–plane forward; bend the left elbow to draw back the left palm, and place the left palm at the right cubital fossa, with the palm down. Eyes look at the right fist.〔Figure 39〕

圖 40

（3）上動不停。身體右轉 90°，重心右移成馬步；
同時，左掌向左下方橫掌推出，置於左膝外側，掌心
斜向下，掌指向前；右拳收抱於腰間，拳心向上；目
視左掌。（圖 40）

(3) Keep the above action, turn the body 90° to the right,
and shift the barycenter rightward into horse stance. At the same
time, push the left palm left downward with the palm horizontal,
then place the left palm at the outer side of the left knee, with the
palm down aslant and the fingers forward; draw back and hold
the right fist on the waist, with the fist–palm up. Eyes look at the
left palm.（Figure 40）

圖 41

15. 馬步沖天炮　Sky cannon in horse stance

(1) 接上勢。身體左轉 90°，重心略上提；同時，左掌變拳，隨身向左、向後擺拳，置於左臀後方，拳背向外，拳眼斜向下；右拳隨身擺至身前方，拳眼向裏，高與胯平。（圖 41）

(1) Follow the above posture, turn the body 90° to the left, and raise the barycenter slightly. At the same time, change the left palm into fist and swing the left fist leftward and back ward with body turn, and place it behind the left buttock, with the back of the fist outward and the fist−hole down aslant; swing the right fist before the body with body turn, keep the fist−hole inward at the hip height. ﹝ Figure 41 ﹞

炮
拳

圖 42

　　(2) 上動不停。身體右轉 90°；同時，右拳隨身向
上、向右擺，置於身前方，拳眼向上，拳心向裏，高
與肩平；左拳繼續向上擺拳，拳心向外，與右拳呈一
直線；目視前方。（圖 42、圖 42 附圖）

炮
拳
套
路
動
作
圖
解

圖 42 附圖

(2) Keep the above action, turn the body 90° to the right. At the same time, swing the right fist upward and rightward with body turn, and place it before the body, keep the palm hole upward and the fist–palm inward, at the shoulders height. Continuously swing the left fist upward, keep the fist–palm outward, in line with the right one. Eyes look forward. (Figure 42, Attached figure 42)

圖 43

（3）上動不停。身體略向右轉，重心略右移；同時，掄左臂向上、向前擺拳，拳心向裏，拳眼向上；右臂向下、向後擺拳，拳心向外，兩拳左前右後呈水平。（圖43、圖 43 附圖）

炮拳套路動作圖解

圖 43 附圖

(3) Keep the above action, turn the body to the right slightly, and move the barycenter rightward slightly. At the same time, brandish the left arm to swing the left fist upward and forward, with the fist–palm inward and fist–hole up. Swing the right fist downward and backward, with the fist–palm outward. Keep the two fists horizontal at left forward and right backward. (Figure 43, Attached figure 43)

圖 44

(4) 上動不停。右拳向前掄拳，與左拳同時收抱於
腰間，拳心向上；目視兩拳。（圖 44、圖 44 附圖）

炮
拳
套
路
動
作
圖
解

圖 44 附圖

(4) Keep the above action, swing the right fist for-ward, and simultaneously draw back and hold it on the waist with the left one. Keep the fist-palm up. Eyes look at the two fists. ﹙Figure 44, Attached figure 44﹚

圖 45

(5) 上動不停。身體起立；兩拳經胸前向左上方沖拳，拳面向上，拳心向裏，右拳在裏高與頭平；左拳在外，略高於右拳；目視左拳。（圖 45、圖 45 附圖）

炮拳套路動作圖解

圖 45 附圖

(5) Keep the above action, raise the body, punch the two fists left upward through the front of the chest, with the fist−planes up and fist−palms inward. Keep the right fist inside, at the head height; keep the left one outside, slightly higher than the right fist. Eyes look at the left fist. (Figure 45, Attached figure 45)

圖46

(6) 上動不停。身體下蹲成馬步；同時，兩臂屈肘回收於胸前，左拳落於左耳側，右拳落於左胸前，兩拳心均向右，拳面均向上；目視右方。（圖46、圖46附圖）

要點：同第4式。

炮拳套路動作圖解

圖 46 附圖

(6) Keep the above action, the bldy squats into horse stance. At the same time, bend the two elbows to draw back the two arms in front of the chest. The left fist falls at the left ear side, while the right one falls in front of the left chest, with both the fist–palms rightward and the fist–planes up. Eyes look rightward. ﹝Figure 46, Attached figure 46﹞

Key points: the same as that of Posture 4.

炮

拳

圖 47

第二段　Section　Two

16. 攔腰雙絕手 Grasp waist for double punches

（1）接上勢。身體右轉 90°，右腳尖外擺，重心前移成右弓步；同時，兩拳變掌，向外、向前弧形探出，兩掌心均向右，掌指均向前，右掌高與肩平，左掌略低於右掌；目視兩掌。（圖 47）

（1）Follow the above posture, turn the body 90° to the right, and turn the right tiptoe outward, shift the barycenter forward into right bow stance. At the same time, change the two fists into palms and stretch them outward and forward in a curve, with both the palms rightward and the fingers forward. Keep the right palm at the shoulders height, and the left one slightly lower than the right one. Eyes look at the two palms.（Figure 47）

圖 48

(2) 上動不停。重心後移，右腳收回，腳尖點地成右虛步；同時，兩掌抓握變拳回收於胸前，右拳在上，拳心向下；左拳在下，拳心向裏；目視前方。（圖 48）

(2) Keep the above action, move the barycenter backward, and draw back the right foot with the tiptoe on ground into right empty stance. At the same time, the two palms clench into fists, and draw them back in front of the chest. Keep the right fist up with the fist–palm down; the left one down with the fist–palm inward. Eyes look forward.（Figure 48）

圖49

（3）上動不停。右腳向前上步，左腳隨即跟步成右
弓步；同時，兩拳向前沖拳，右拳眼向下，拳心向
外，高與肩平；左拳拳心向裏，略低於右拳；目視前
方。（圖49）

要點：上步迅速，沖拳要抖肩發力，力達拳面。

(3) Keep the above action, the right foot steps for-ward,
then the left one follows up into right bow stance. At the same
time, punch the two fists forward. Keep the right fist-hole down
and the fist-palm outward, at the shoulders level; the left
fist-palm inward, slightly lower than the right fist. Eyes look
forward.〔Figure 49〕

Key points: quickly step forward. When punching the fist,
snap the shoulders to release force that shall reach the fist-face.

炮拳套路動作圖解

圖 50

17. 抬腿小提鞋
Raise the leg to lift small shoe

(1) 接上勢。兩拳變掌，左掌從右腕下穿出與右掌交叉；右掌心向下，掌指向前；左掌心向外，掌指向上；目視前方。（圖 50）

(1) Follow the above posture, change the two fists into palms, thread the left palm out form under the right wrist, and cross it with the right one. Keep the right palm downward and the fingers forward; the left palm outward and the fingers up. Eyes look forward. (Figure 50)

圖 51

(2) 上動不停。身體略右轉，左腳跟提起；同時，兩掌翻腕絞手，右掌心向上，掌指向前；左掌心向下，掌指向後；目視前方。（圖 51）

(2) Keep the above action, turn the body to the right slightly and raise the left tiptoe. At the same time, turn over the two wrists to twist the two hands, keep the right palm upward and the fingers forward; the left one down and the fingers backward. Eyes look forward. 〔Figure 51〕

圖 52

（3）上動不停。身體右轉 90°，右腳獨立，腳尖外擺，左腿提起向左上方側踹腿；同時，兩掌變拳抱於胸前，右拳在下，左拳在上，兩拳心相對；目視左腳。（圖52）

要點：右腿獨立穩固，左踹腿要高，身體右傾接近水平。

(3) Keep the above action, turn the body 90° to the right, stand on the right foot with the tiptoe outward, raise the left leg to kick sideways left upward. At the same time, change the two palms into fists and hold the two fists in front of the chest. Keep the right fist down and the left one up, with the two fist–palms opposite. Eyes look at the left foot.（Figure 52）

Key points: stand on the right leg firmly, the left kick shall be high, and the body shall slant rightward, nearly horizontal.

圖53

18. 落步右拐肘
Land step and bend right elbow

（1）接上勢。身體左轉90°，左腳向前落步成左弓步；同時，左拳變掌外摟，翻掌成掌心向上，掌指向前，高與肩平；右拳抱於腰間，拳心向上；目視左掌。（圖53）

(1) Follow the above posture, the body turns 90° to the left, and the left foot falls forward into left bow step. At the same time, change the left fist into palm and grab it outward, turn the palm over into the palm upward and the fingers forward, at the shoulders level; hold the right fist on the waist, with the fist–palm up. Eyes look at the left palm.（Figure 53）

圖 54

（2）上動不停。身體略左轉；同時，右臂屈肘向左下斜擊，高與肩平；左掌向裏迎擊右肘外側；目視右肘。（圖 54）

要點：拐肘要蹬腿擰腰，肩催肘發。

(2) Keep the above action, turn the body to the left slightly. At the same time, bend the right elbow to strike left downward aslant, at the shoulders height; the left palm counterpunch the outer side of the right elbow. Eyes look at the right elbow. (Figure 54)

Key points: for bending the elbow, straighten the leg and twist the waist, move the shoulder sent elbow to release force.

圖 55

19. 轉身雙絕雙分腿　Double punches and double separations with body turn

（1）接上勢。右轉身 180°，重心前移成右弓步；同時，右拳變掌，兩掌一起從胸前向右膝前方探出，掌心向下，掌指向前；目視兩掌。（圖 55）

（1）Follow the above posture, turn the body 180° to the right. Move the barycenter forward into right bow stance. At the same time, change the right fist into palm, and stretch the two palms together to the front of the right knee though the front of the chest, with the palms downward and the fingers forward. Eyes look at the two palms.（Figure 55）

圖 56

(2)上動不停。重心後移，右膝提起，左腿獨立；
同時，兩掌抓握變拳抱於腰間，兩拳心均向上；目視
前方。（圖 56）

(2) Keep the above action, shift the barycenter backward,
raise the right knee and stand on the left leg. At the same time,
clench the two palms into fists and hold them on the waist, with
both the fist-palms up. Eyes look forward. (Figure 56)

圖 57

（3）上動不停。右腳向前落步，左腳隨即跟步，重心落於兩腿間；同時，兩拳向前平沖，兩拳眼相對，拳心均向下，高與肩平；目視前方。（圖 57）

(3) Keep the above action, the right leg falls forward, then the left one follows up, and the barycenter moves between the two legs. At the same time, horizontally punch the two fists forward, with the two fist-holes opposite and both the fist-palms down, at the shoulders height. Eyes look forward. ﹝Figure 57﹞

炮拳套路動作圖解

圖 58

(4) 上動不停。右腳向前上一小步，左腳向前併步，身體下蹲成蹲步；同時，兩拳從上向下劈拳，置於兩膝外側，兩拳眼均向裏，拳面均向下；目視前下方。（圖58）

(4) Keep the above action, the right foot takes a small step forward, and the left one steps forward, put the feet together and squat into squatting stance. At the same time, hack the two fists from upward to downward, and place them at the outer side of the two knees, with both the fist−holes inward and the fist−planes down. Eyes look downward ahead. (Figure 58)

圖 59

20. 起身雙風貫耳　Raise to strike the opponent's ears with both fists

（1）接上勢。重心微上提；同時，兩拳分別從身體兩側向上抬起，拳心均向下，拳眼均向前，高與肩平；目視前方。（圖 59、圖 59 附圖）

圖 59 附圖

(1) Follow the above posture, raise the barycenter slightly. At the same time, simultaneously lift the two fists from both sides of the body respectively. Keep both the fist-palm downward and fist-holes forward, at shoulders height. Eyes look forward. (Figure 59, Attached figure 59)

炮
拳

圖 60

（2）上動不停。身體起立；同時，兩臂屈肘，兩拳外旋，從身體兩側向裏合擊，兩拳輪相對，拳心均向裏，高與肩平；目視前方。（圖 60）

要點：兩拳合力向裏合擊，動作要迅猛有力，力達拳輪。

(2) Keep the above action, raise the body. At the same time, bend the elbows, rotate the two fists outward to jointly strike inward from both sides of the body, with the two fist-wheels opposite and both the fist-palms inward, at the shoulders height. Eyes look forward.〔Figure 60〕

Key points: the two fists jointly strike inward with resultant force, and the action shall be swift and forceful, with the force reaching the fist-wheel.

炮拳套路動作圖解

圖 61

21. 起手迎面錘
Raise hand and strike face with hammer

（1）接上勢。左腳向前上步，重心前移成左弓步；同時，左拳變掌向前探出，掌指向前，掌心向裏，高與肩平；右拳收抱於腰間；目視左掌。（圖 61）

(1) Follow the above posture, the left foot steps for-ward, and move the barycenter forward into left bow stance. At the same time, change the left fist into palm and stretch the left palm forward, with the fingers forward and the palm inward, at the shoulders height; draw back the right fist and hold it on the waist. Eyes look at the left palm.（Figure 61）

圖62

（2）上動不停。左掌翻掌成掌心向上；同時，右拳從後向前掄起栽擊於左掌心，兩臂微屈；目視右拳。（圖62）

要點：掄臂迅速有力，栽拳力達拳面。

(2) Follow the above posture, turn over the left palm with palm up. At the same time, swing right fist from rear to forward to pound on the centre of left palm, both arms bent slightly. Look at the right fist.〔Figure 62〕

Key points: brandishing the arm shall be quick and forceful, with the strength of downward punch reaching the striking surfaceof the fist.

圖 63

22. 轉身雲頂七星
Turn body and cloud top into seven-star

（1）接上勢。身體起立右轉 90°；同時，右拳變掌，兩掌一起經胸前向右、向上雲托，右掌置於頭右側方，高與頭頂平；左掌置於頭頂上方，兩掌心均向上，掌指均向右；目視右掌。（圖 63）

（1）Follow the above posture, raise the body and turn 90° to the right. At the same time, cloud the two palms together right-ward and upward through the front of the chest, and place the right palm at the right side of the head, at the head top height; the left one above the head top. Keep both the palms upward and the fingers rightward. Eyes look at the right palm. （Figure 63）

炮
拳

圖 64

(2) 上動不停。右腳尖外擺，左腳跟離地，身體右
轉 90°；同時，兩掌經頭頂向後雲托，隨即下落成拳收
抱於腰間，拳心向上；目視前方。（圖 64）

(2) Keep the above action, the right tiptoe turns outward, the
left foot leaves the ground, and the body turns 90° to the right. At
the same time, the two palms cloudlift backward through the
head top, then falls, draw back and hold them on the waist, with
the fist–palm up. Eyes look forward.〔Figure 64〕

炮拳套路動作圖解

圖 65

（3）上動不停。左腳向前上步成丁步；同時，右拳向前平沖，拳心向下，拳眼向左，高與肩平；左臂屈肘前撐，拳面抵於右肘內側，拳心向下；目視右拳。（圖65）

要點：同第6式。

(3) Keep the above action, the left foot steps forward into T-shape stance. At the same time, horizontally punch the right fist forward, with the fist-palm down and fist-hole leftward, at the shoulders height; bend the left elbow to support the left arm forward, keep the fist-plane close to the inner side of the right elbow, with the fist-palm down. Eyes look at the right fist. (Figure 65)

Key points: the same as that of Posture 6.

圖 66

23. 轉身單鞭　Single whip with body turn

（1）接上勢。身體左轉 90°，左腳向左橫跨一步成馬步；同時，兩拳外旋，屈肘合於胸前併齊，拳心向裏，高與肩平；目視兩拳。（圖 66、圖 66 附圖）

炮拳套路動作圖解

圖 66 附圖

(1) Follow the above posture, the body turns 90° to the left, and the left foot strides a step leftward into horse stance. At the same time, rotate the two fists outward, bend the elbows to combine them in front of the chest and put them together. Keep the fist–palms inward at the shoulders height. Eyes look at the two fists. ﹝ Figure 66, Attached figure 66 ﹞

炮
拳

圖 67

　(2) 上動不停。兩拳分別向身體兩側平沖，拳心均向下，拳眼均向前，高與肩平；目視左方。（圖 67）

　要點：同第 7 式。

　(2) Keep the above action, horizontally punch the two fists to both sides of the body respectively, with both the fist–palms down and the fist–holes forward, at the shoulders height. Eyes look leftward.〔Figure 67〕

　Key points: the same as that of Posture 7.

圖68

24. 五花虎抱頭
Swing arms into tiger holds head

(1) 接上勢。身體略向右轉，重心稍上提；同時，左臂隨身向上、向前直臂擺拳於胸前，拳心向裏，拳眼向上；右臂向下、向後擺拳，拳眼向上，兩臂呈水平。（圖68、圖 68 附圖）

圖 68 附圖

(1) Follow the above posture, turn the body to the right slightly, and raise the barycenter slightly. At the same time, swing the left fist upward and forward in front of the chest with the arms straight and body turn, keep the fist–palm inward and fist–hole up. Swing the right fist downward and backward, with the fist–hole up. Keep the two arms horizontal. 〔 Figure 68, Attached figure 68 〕

炮拳套路動作圖解

圖 69

(2) 上動不停。身體略向左轉，重心移至左腿；同時，右臂隨身向上、向前直臂擺拳，置於身體左前方，拳心向裏，拳眼向上；左臂向下、向後擺拳，拳眼向上，兩臂呈水平；目視右拳。（圖 69）

(2) Keep the above action, turn the body to the left slightly, and shift the barycenter to the left leg. At the same time, swing the right fist upward and forward with the arm straight and body turn, and place it before the left of the body. Keep the fist–palm inward and fist–hole up; swing the left fist downward and backward, with the fist–hole up. Keep the two arms horizontal. Eyes look at the right fist.〔Figure 69〕

圖 70

（3）上動不停。身體略向右轉，重心移至右腿，左
腳收於右腳內側，腳尖點地成左丁步；同時，右臂隨
身向右、向上擺，架拳於頭前上方，拳心向前，拳眼
向下；左臂隨身向前、向裏擺拳，屈臂盤肘，左拳落
於腹前，拳心向下，拳眼向裏；目視左方。（圖 70、
圖 70 附圖）

炮
拳
套
路
動
作
圖
解

圖 70 圖

(3) Keep the above action, turn the body to the right slightly, and shift the barycenter to the right leg. Draw back the left leg to the inner side of the right one, with the tiptoe on ground into left T-stance. At the same time, swing the right arm rightward and upward with body turn, and place the right fist above the fore part of the head, with the fist-palm forward and fist-hole down. Swing the left fist forward and inward with body turn, bend the left arm and cross the left elbow, then the left fist falls in front of the abdomen, with the fist-palm down and fist-hole inward. Eyes look leftward. (Figure 70, Attached figure 70)

圖 71

25. 搖身三臥枕　Sway body to rest on the pillow three times

(1) 接上勢。身體略向右轉，左腳向左開一步；同時，左拳從胸前向前上方直臂掄起，拳心向右，拳眼向上，略高於肩；右拳隨身向後、向下掄拳，拳心向下，拳眼向外；目視左拳。（圖71）

炮
拳
套
路
動
作
圖
解

(1) Follow the above posture, turn the body to the right slightly. The left foot takes a step leftward. At the same time, swing the left fist upward ahead with the arm straight through the front of the chest, keep the fist–palm rightward and fist–hole upward, slightly higher than the shoulders; swing the right fist backward and downward with body turn, keep the fist–palm down and fist–hole outward. Eyes look at the left fist. (Figure 71)

炮拳

圖72

(2) 上動不停。身體左轉 90°；同時，右拳隨身向上、向前掄起，置於頭右前方，拳心向前；左臂隨身向左、向下掄拳，置於左胯側，拳心向外，拳面向下。（圖72）

(2) Keep the above action, turn the body 90° to the left. At the same time, swing the right fist upward and forward with body turn, and place it before the right part of the head, with the fist–palm forward; swing the left arm leftward and downward with body turn, and place it at the left crotch side, with the fist–palm outward and the fist–plane down. ﹝ Figure 72 ﹞

炮拳套路動作圖解

圖73

(3) 上動不停。右腳向前一步，身體左轉 90°下蹲
成馬步；同時，左拳由外向上、向裏畫拳，屈肘置於
左肩前，拳眼向裏，拳面斜向下；右拳從右向前落於
襠前，拳心向裏，拳面向下；目視右拳。（圖 73）

(3) Keep the above action, the right foot takes a step
forward, the body 90° to the left and squats into horse stance. At
the same time, swing the left fist from outward to upward and
inward, bend the left elbow to place the left fist before the left
shoulder; with the fist-hole inward and the fist-plane down
aslant, the right fist falls in front of the crotch from rightward to
forward, with the fist-palm inward and fist-plane down. Eyes
look at the right fist. 〔 Figure 73 〕

炮

拳

圖 74

　　(4)上動不停。重心右移成弓步，身體微向右傾；
同時，左拳經胸前向下栽拳於襠前，拳心向裏，拳面
向下；右臂屈肘向上提，抱拳於右胸前，拳心向裏，
拳面向上；目視左方。（圖 74）

　　(4) Keep the above action, move the barycenter rightward
into bow stance, and slightly slant the body rightward. At the
same time, punch the left fist downward in front of the crotch
through the front of the chest, with the fist-palm inward and
fist-plane down; bend the right elbow to lift the right arm, hold
the right fist in front of the chest, with the fist-palm inward and
the fist-plane up. Eyes look leftward.（Figure 74）

炮拳套路動作圖解

圖 75

（5）上動不停。身體略向左轉，重心移至左腿；同時，右臂伸直向右擺拳，拳心向下，高與肩平；左拳直臂擺於身後；目視右方。（圖 75）

(5) Keep the above action, turn the body to the left slightly, and shift the barycenter to the left leg. At the same time, stretch the right arm straight to swing the right fist rightward, with the fist－palm down, at the shoulders height; swing the left fist behind the body with the arm straight. Eyes look rightward. (Figure 75)

圖 76

　　⑹上動不停。右腳尖外擺，身體略右轉，右腳回收落於左腳內側；同時，右拳走下弧，經胸前向上、向右掄拳，拳心向裏，略高於肩；目視前方。（圖76）

　　⑹ Keep the above action, the right tiptoe turns outward, and the body slightly turns to the right, the right foot withdraws and lands to the inner side of the left one. At the same time, swing the right fist upward and rightward in an lower curve through the front of the chest, with the fist–palm inward, slightly higher that the shoulders. Eyes look forward.（Figure 76）

圖 77

(7) 上動不停。左腳向前上一步，身體右轉 180°；同時，右拳隨身繼續向右上方掄擺，拳心向裏，拳眼向上；左拳隨身走上弧，掄擺於身體左後方，拳心斜向下，兩臂呈水平；目視右拳。（圖 77）

(7) Keep the above action, the left foot takes a step forward, and the body turns 180° to the right. At the same time, continue to swing the right fist right upward with body turn, keep the fist–palm inward and fist–hole upward; swing the left one behind the left of the body in an upper curve with body turn, keep the fist –palm down aslant. Keep the two arms horizontal. Eyes look at the right fist.（Figure 77）

炮拳

圖 78

(8)上動不停。兩腿下蹲移成馬步；同時，左拳下擺於襠前，拳心向裏，拳面向下；右拳屈臂置於右肩前，拳眼向裏。（圖 78）

(8) Keep the above action, the two legs squat into horse stance. At the same time, swing the left fist downward in front of the crotch, with the fist-palm inward and the fist-face down, bend the right arm to place the right fist before the right shoulder, with the fist-hole inward.（Figure 78）

炮拳套路動作圖解

圖 79

(9)上動不停。重心左移，身體微向左傾；同時，
右拳經胸前向下栽拳於襠前，拳心向裏，拳面向下；
左臂屈肘向上提，抱拳於左胸前，拳心向裏，拳面向
上；目視右方。（圖 79）

(9) Keep the above action, move the barycenter leftward,
and slightly slant the body leftward. At the same time, punch the
right fist downward in front of the crotch through the front of the
chest, with the fist–palm inward and the fist–plane down; bend
the left elbow to lift the left arm, then hold the left fist in front of
the left chest, with the fist–palm inward and the fist–plane up.
Eyes look rightward.（Figure 79）

圖 80

（10）上動不停。身體略向右轉，重心移至右腿；同時，左臂伸直，在胸前向左上方擺拳，拳眼向上，高與頭頂平；右拳擺於身後；目視左方。（圖 80）

(10) Keep the above action, turn the body to the right slightly, and move the barycenter to the right leg. At the same time, stretch the left arm straight to swing the left fist left upward in front of the chest, with the fist–hole up, at the head top level; swing the right fist behind the body. Eyes look leftward. 〔Figure 80〕

炮拳套路動作圖解

圖 81

⑾ 上動不停。左腳回收落於右腳內側；同時，左
拳下擺於左膝外側，拳心向裏；右拳向上、向前擺
拳，高與頭頂平；目視前方。（圖 81）

⑾ Keep the above action, the left foot with draws and falls
to the inner side of the right foot. At the same time, swing the
left fist downward to the outer side of the left knee, with the
fist–palm inward; swing the right one upward and forward, at the
head top level. Eyes look forward.（Figure 81）

炮
拳

圖82

⑿ 上動不停。右腳向前上一步，身體左轉 90°，
身體下蹲成馬步；同時，左拳隨身向外、向上、向裏
畫拳，屈肘置於左肩前，拳眼向裏，拳面斜向下；右
拳從右向前落於襠前，拳心向裏，拳面向下；目視右
拳。（圖82）

⑿ Keep the above action, the right foot takes a step
forward, and the body turns 90° to the left. The body squats into
horse stance. At same time, swing the left fist outward, upward
and inward with body turn, bend the left elbow to place the left
fist before the left shoulder, with the fist–hole inward and the
fist–plane downward aslant; the right fist falls to the front of the
crotch from rightward to forward, with the fist–palm inward and
the fist–plane down. Eyes look at the right fist.（Figure 82）

炮拳套路動作圖解

圖 83

⒀上動不停。重心右移成右弓步，身體微向右
傾；同時，左拳經胸前向下栽拳於襠前，拳心向裏，
拳面向下；右臂屈肘向上提，抱拳於右胸前，拳心向
裏，拳面向上；目視左方。（圖 83）

要點：整個動作要快速連貫，協調一致。

⒀ Keep the above action, move the barycenter rightward
into right bow stance, and slant the body right-ward slightly. At
the same time, punch the left fist down-ward to the front of the
crotch through the front of the chest, with the fist-palm inward
and fist-plane down; bend the right elbow to raise the right arm,
then hold the right fist in front of the right chest, with the
fist-palm inward and fist-plane up. Eyes look leftward.（Figure
83）

Key points: the whole action shall be quick and coherent,
harmonious and consistent.

炮拳

圖 84

26. 轉身窩心捶
Turn body to punch heart with hammer

（1）接上勢。身體左轉 90°，重心前移成左弓步；同時，右拳經腰間向前沖拳，拳心向上，略低於肩；左拳變掌，向外、向上畫弧，再向裏屈肘按掌，掌心貼於右肘窩處；目視右拳。（圖 84）

炮拳套路動作圖解

(1) Follow the above posture, turn the body 90° to the left, and move the barycenter forward into left bow stance. At the same time, punch the right fist forward through the waist, with the fist–palm up, slightly lower that the shoulders; change the left fist into palm and draw a circle outward and upward with the left palm, then bend the left elbow and press the left palm inward, keep the palm close to the right cubital fossa. Eyes look at the right fist. (Figure 84)

炮

拳

圖 85

(2) 上動不停。身體右轉 90°，重心右移成馬步；
同時，右拳收抱於腰間，拳心向上；左掌向左下方橫
掌推出，置於左膝外側，掌心斜向下，掌指向前；目
視左掌。（圖 85）

(2) Keep the above action, turn the body to 90° to the right,
and shift the barycenter rightward into horse stance. At the same
time, draw back and hold the right fist on the waist, with the
fist–palm up; push the left palm left downward with the palm
horizontal, and place it at the outer side of the left knee, with the
palm outward aslant and the fingers forward. Eyes look at the
left palm.〔Figure 85〕

炮拳套路動作圖解

圖 86

27. 倒步沖天炮
Sky cannon with backward step

（1）接上勢。身體略左轉，右腳經左腳後向左插步；同時，左掌變拳，擺於身體左後方；右拳從外向前、向左擺於左胯前，拳心向裏；目視右拳。（圖86）

(1) Follow the above posture, turn the body to the left slightly. The right foot makes cross stance to the left behind the left foot. At the same time, change the left palm into fist and swing the left fist behind the left part of the body; swing the right fist in front of the left hip outward to forward and leftward with the fist–palm inward. Eyes look at the right fist.〔Figure 86〕

炮拳

圖 87

（2）上動不停。左腳向左橫跨一步，重心移至兩腿間；同時，掄右臂向上、向右擺拳，拳眼向上；左拳繼續向後、向上擺，拳心向外，拳眼向上，兩臂呈水平；目視右拳。（圖 87）

(2) Keep the above action, the left foot strides a step leftward and transfer the barycenter between two legs. At the same time, brandish the right arm to swing the right fist upward and rightward with the fist—hole up; continuously swing the left fist backward and upward with the fist—palm outward and fist—hole up. Keep two arms horizontal. Eyes look at the right fist.（Figure 87）

炮拳套路動作圖解

圖 88

(3) 上動不停。身體右轉 90°，重心移至右腿；同時，左臂隨身向上、向前擺拳，拳心向裏；右臂隨身向下、向後擺拳，拳心向外，兩拳眼均向上，兩臂呈水平；目視左拳。（圖 88）

(3) Keep the above action, turn the body 90° to the right and transfer the barycenter to the right leg. At the same time, swing the left fist upward and forward with body turn and fist-palm inward; swing the right fist downward and backward with fist-palm outward and body turn. Keep two fist-holes up and two arms at the same level. Eyes look at the left fist. 〔Figure 88 〕

炮

拳

圖 89

　　(4) 上動不停。身體左轉 90°，重心下移成馬步；同時，左拳抱於腰間；右臂隨身向上、向前掄臂，抱拳於左腰間，兩拳心均向上；目視兩拳。（圖 89）

　　(4) Keep the above action, turn the body 90° to the left and transfer the barycenter downward into horse stance. At the same time, hold the left fist on the waist; swing the right arm upward and forward with the body, then hold the right fist on the left waist with two fist–palms up. Eyes look at the two fists.〔Figure 89〕

炮拳套路動作圖解

圖 90

(5) 上動不停。身體起立；兩拳經胸前向左上方沖拳，拳面向上，拳心向裏，右拳在裏高與頭平；左拳在外，略高於右拳；目視兩拳。（圖 90）

(5) Keep the above action, the body stands up, two fists strike left upward through the front of the chest, with the fist-face upward and fist-palm inward. Keep the right fist inside at the head level; the left fist outside higher than the right fist. Eyes look at two fists. 〔Figure 90〕

炮
拳

圖91

（6）上動不停。身體下蹲成馬步；同時，兩臂屈肘回收於胸前，左拳落於左耳側，右拳落於左胸前，兩拳心均向右，拳面均向上；目視右方。（圖91）

要點：同第4式。

(6) Keep the above action, the body squats into horse stance. At the same time, bend two elbows to draw the two arms back before the chest. The left fist falls at the left ear side and the right one falls before the left chest with two fist–palms rightward and the fist–planes up. Eyes look rightward.（Figure 91）

Key points: the same as that of Posture 4.

炮拳套路動作圖解

圖 92

第三段 Section Three

28. 轉身單叉 Single split with body turn

(1) 接上勢。右臂經胸前向下、向右擺拳，拳心向下，高與肩平；同時，左拳向左後方掄擺，拳心向後，拳眼向下；目視右方。（圖 92）

(1) Follow the above posture, swing the right fist downward and rightward through the front of the chest, with the fist—palm down at the shoulders height. At the same time, the left fist swings left backward with the fist—palm backward and fist—hole down. Eyes look rightward.（Figure 92）

圖 93

（2）上動不停。身體右轉 180°，雙腳蹬地跳起；同時，右臂在胸前掄一立圓，抱拳於腰間；左臂屈肘，左拳變掌收於胸前，掌心向右，掌指向上；目視左下方。（圖 93、圖 93 附圖）

圖 93 附圖

(2) Keep the above action, turn the body $180°$ to the right two feet press against the ground to jump up. At the same time, the right arm swings an upright circle before the chest, then hold the right fist on the waist. Bend the left elbow, change the left fist into palm and draw the palm back before the chest with the palm rightward and fingers up. Eyes look left downward. (Figure 93 Attached figure 93)

圖 94

(3) 上動不停。右腳落地，左腳隨即向左鏟出，身體下蹲成左仆步；同時，左掌從胸前沿左腿向左切掌，掌心向下，掌緣向左；目視左掌。（圖 94、圖 94 附圖）

要點：雙腳跳換步要輕靈快捷，仆步和切掌同時完成。

炮
拳
套
路
動
作
圖
解

圖 94 附圖

(3) Keep the above action, the right foot lands to the ground, then the left foot shovels leftward and the body squats into a left crouch stance. At the same time, the left palm cuts leftward from the front of the chest along the left leg, with palm down and palm edge leftward. Eyes look at the left palm. (Figure 94, Attached figure 94)

Key points: two feet jumping to change step shall be light and prompt; the crouch stance and palm cutting shall be completed simultaneously.

炮拳

圖 95

29. 起身拐肘　Rise body and bend elbow

接上勢。身體略向左轉，重心前移成左弓步；同時，右臂屈肘，由後向左下方斜擊；左掌迎擊右前臂外側；目視前方。（圖95）

要點：蹬腿擰腰，以肩催動右肘。

Follow the above posture, turn the body to the left slightly. Transfer the barycenter forward into left bow stance. At the same time, bend the right elbow to strike from backward to left downward aslant; the left palm counterpunches the outer side of the right forearm. Eyes look forward. ﹝Figure 95﹞

Key points: kick the leg and twist the waist; hasten the right elbow by shoulder.

圖 96

30. 轉身雙絕雙分腿 Double punches and double separations with body turn

（1）接上勢。右轉身 180°，重心前移成右弓步；同時，右拳變掌，兩掌一起從胸前向右膝前方探出，掌心向下，掌指向前；目視兩掌。（圖 96）

(1) Follow the above posture, turn the body 180° to the right. Transfer the barycenter forward into right bow stance. At the same time, change the right fist into palm, stretch the two palms together from the front of the chest to the front of the right knee, with the palm down and fingers forward. Eyes look at the two palms.（Figure 96）

圖 97

（2）上動不停。重心後移，右膝提起，左腿獨立；同時，兩掌抓握變拳，收抱於腰間，拳心均向上；目視前方。（圖97）

（2）Keep the above action, transfer the barycenter backward, lift the right knee and stand on the left leg. At the same time, two palms grab into fists, draw back and hold them on the waist with both fist-palms up. Eyes look forward. （Figure 97）

圖 98

（3）上動不停。右腳向前跨一步，左腳隨即跟步，重心落於兩腿間；同時，兩拳向前平沖，兩拳眼相對，拳心均向下，高與肩平；目視前方。（圖 98）

(3) Keep the above action, the right foot stride a step forward, then the left one follows up with the barycenter falling between two legs. At the same time, two fists strike forward horizontally with two fist-holes opposite and fist-palms down at the shoulders level. Eyes look forward.（Figure 98）

圖 99

（4）上動不停。右腳向前上一小步，左腳向前併步，身體下蹲成蹲步；同時，兩拳從上向下劈拳，落於兩腿外側，兩拳眼均向裏，拳面均向下；目視前下方。（圖 99）

要點：同第 19 式。

(4) Keep the above action, the right foot takes a small step forward and the left one follows up to bring feet together, squat the body into squatting stance. At the same time, two fists hack from upward to downward and fall at the outer sides of the two legs, with both the fist-holes inward and fist-plane down. Eyes look down-ward ahead.（Figure 99）

Key points: the same as that of Posture 19.

炮拳套路動作圖解

圖 100

31. 起身雙風貫耳　Rise body to strike the opponent's ears with both fists

（1）接上勢。重心微上提；同時，兩拳分別從身體兩側向上抬起，拳心均向下，拳眼均向前，高與肩平；目視前方。（圖 100）

（1）Follow the above posture, raise the barycenter slightly. At the same time, lift two fists from fist-palms of the body respectively with fist-palms down and fist-holes forward at the shoulders height. Eyes look forward.（Figure 100）

炮
拳

圖 101

(2) 上動不停。身體起立；同時，兩臂屈肘，兩拳外旋，從身兩側向裏合擊，兩拳輪相對，拳心均向裏，高與肩平；目視前方。（圖 101）

要點：同第 20 式。

(2) Keep the above action, the body stands up. At the same time, bend the elbows, swing two fists outward from both sides of the body, with the two fist-wheels opposite and fist-palms inward at the shoulders height. Eyes look forward.（Figure 101）

Key points: the same as that of Posture 20.

圖102

32. 劈腿左斜形
Splitting leg with left diagonal posture

(1) 接上勢。右腳向前上一步；同時，右拳收抱於腰間，拳心向上；左拳上抬置於左耳側，拳眼向後；目視前方。（圖102）

(1) Follow the above posture, the right foot takes a step forward. At the same time, draw back and hold the right fist on the waist with the fist-palm up; raise the left fist and place it at the left ear side with the fist-hole backward. Eyes look forward. 〔Figure 102〕

炮

拳

圖 103

(2) 上動不停。重心前移至右腿，左腿抬起向前正
踢腿；同時，左拳從上向下劈拳落於左胯側，拳心向
裏。（圖 103）

(2) Keep the above action, transfer the barycenter forward
to the right leg. Lift the left leg and kick it up ahead. At the same
time, the left fist hacks from upward to downward and falls at
the left hip side with the fist-palm inward.（Figure 103）

圖 104

(3) 上動不停。身體右轉 90°，左腳向左側落地成
馬步；同時，兩臂交叉抱於胸前，左拳在外，右拳在
裏，兩拳心均朝裏；目視兩拳。（圖 104）

(3) Keep the above action, turn the body 90° to the right,
the left foot falls to the left side into horse-stance. At the same
time, cross the two arms and hold them before the chest. Keep
the left fist outside and the right one inside, with two fist-palms
inward. Eyes look at the two fists.（Figure 104）

圖 105

(4) 上動不停。左腳尖外擺，身體左轉 90°，重心前移成左弓步；同時，左拳隨身向後撐拳，右拳向前撐拳，兩臂微屈，拳眼相對，兩拳心均向下，高與肩平；目視前方。（圖 105）

要點：左踢腿要高，與左劈拳同時進行。

(4) Keep the above action, the left tiptoe turns out–ward and the body turns 90° to the left, transfer the barycenter forward into left bow stance. At the same time, support the left fist backward with the body, and support the right one forward. Two arms bend slightly with the fist–holes opposite and fist–palms down at the shoulders level. Eyes look forward.（Figure 105）

Key point: the left leg kicking shall be high and done with the left fist hacking simultaneously.

炮拳套路動作圖解

圖 106

33. 劈腿右斜形
Splitting leg with right diagonal posture

（1）接上勢。弓步不動；左拳收於腰間，拳心向上；右拳向上、向後擺拳於右耳側，拳眼向後；目視前方。（圖 106）

（1）Follow the above posture, keep the bow step, and hold the left fist on the waist with the fist–palm up; swing the right fist upward and backward to the right ear side with the fist–hole backward. Eyes look forward.（Figure 106）

炮
拳
．

圖 107

(2) 上動不停。重心前移至左腿，右腿抬起向前正
踢腿；同時，右拳經右腿外側向下劈拳，落於身右
側，拳心向裏，拳面向下；目視右腳。（圖 107）

(2) Keep the above action, transfer the barycenter forward
onto the left leg, lift the right leg and kick up ahead. At the same
time, the right fist hacks downward through the outer side of the
right leg and falls at the right side of the body, with the fist–palm
inward and fist–plane down. Eyes look at the right foot. 〔 Figure
107 〕

炮拳套路動作圖解

圖 108

（3）上動不停。身體左轉 90°，右腳向右落步成馬步；同時，兩拳從外向裏畫弧，交叉合抱於胸前，右拳在外，左拳在裏，兩拳心均向裏；目視兩拳。（圖108、圖 108 附圖）

炮
拳

圖 108 附圖

(3) Keep the above action, turn the body 90° to the left, the right foot lands rightward into horse stance. At the same time, the two fists draw a curve from outward to inward, then cross and hold them before the chest. Keep the right fist outside and the left one inside, with both fist–palms inward. Eyes look at the two fists.（Figure 108, Attached figure 108）

炮拳套路動作圖解

圖 109

(4) 上動不停。右腳尖外擺，身體右轉 90°，重心前移成右弓步；同時，右拳隨身向後撐拳，左拳向前撐拳，兩臂微屈，拳眼相對，兩拳心均向下，高與肩平；目視前方。（圖 109）

要點：同第 12 式。

(4) Keep the above action, turn the right tiptoe out−ward and the body 90° to the right, transfer the barycenter forward into right bow stance. At the same time, support the right fist backward with the body, and support the left fist forward. Bend two arms slightly, with the fist−holes opposite and fist−palms down at the shoulders level. Eyes look forward.（Figure 109）

Key point: the same as that of Posture 12.

炮
拳

圖 110

34.恨腳海底炮　Stamping the foot for cannon at the bottom of sea

(1) 接上勢。身體左轉 180°成跪步；同時，左拳變掌，隨身向左、向後擺掌，置於頭後上方，掌心向上，掌指向右；右拳隨身向下、向裏裹右腿，置於左腿內側，拳心向裏，拳面向下；目視右拳。（圖110、圖110附圖）

圖 110 附圖

(1) Follow the above posture, turn the body to the left by 180° into kneel stance. At the same time, change the left fist into palm and swing it with the body leftward and backward, and place it above the head backward, with the palm up and fingers rightward. The right fist wraps the right leg downward and inward with the body, and place it at the inner side of the left leg with the fist–palm inward and fist–plane down.

Eyes look at the right fist. (Figure 110, Attached figure 110)

炮
拳

圖 111

（2）上動不停。左腿獨立，右膝提起，腳尖內扣；
同時，左掌向後、向下擺掌，落於左胯側，掌心向
裏，掌指向下；右拳經胸前向上提至右胸前，拳眼向
裏，拳心向下。（圖 111、圖 111 附圖）

圖 111 附圖

(2) Keep the above action, stand on the left leg and lift the right knee with the tiptoe turned inward. At the same time, the left palm swings backward and downward and lands at the left hip side, with the palm inward and fingers down. Raise the right fist upward to the front of the right chest through the front of the chest, with the fist–hole inward and fist–palm down. 〔 Figure 111, Attached figure 111 〕

圖 112

(3) 上動不停。右腳落步震腳，身體下蹲成蹲步；
同時，左臂屈肘，左掌上提成掌心向上；右拳翻腕向
下砸拳，拳背落於左掌心，發「咿」聲；目視右拳。
（圖 112、圖 112 附圖）

炮
拳
套
路
動
作
圖
解

圖 112 附 圖

(3) Keep the above action, the right foot lands and stamps, the body squats into squatting stance. At the same time, bend the left arm and lift the left palm with the palm up; turn over the right wrist and hack the right fist downward, with back of the fist falls in the left palm, send "Yee" sound. Eyes look at the right fist (Figure 112, Attached figure 112)

炮
拳

圖 113

35. 上步兩捶　Step forward and punch twice

（1）接上勢。身體右轉 90°，右腳向前上一步成右弓步；同時，右拳向前平沖，拳心向下，拳眼向裏，高與肩平；左掌變拳抱於腰間，拳心向上；目視右拳。（圖 113）

(1) Follow the above posture, turn the body 90° to the right. The right foot takes a step forward into right bow stance. At the same time, the right fist strikes forward horizontally, with the fist-palm down and fist-hole inward at the shoulders height; change the left palm into fist and hold the fist on the waist with the fist-palm up. Eyes look at the right fist.（Figure 113）

炮
拳
套
路
動
作
圖
解

圖 114

（2）上動不停。身微右轉，左腳向前跨一步成左弓步；同時，左拳向前平沖，拳心向下，高與肩平；右拳收抱於腰間，拳心向上；目視左拳。（圖 114）

要點：整個動作要連貫迅速，抖肩發力，力達拳面。

（2）Keep the above action, turn the body to the right slightly. The left foot takes a stride forward into left bow stance. At the same time, the left fist strikes forward horizontally with the fist-palm down at the shoulders level; draw back and hold the right fist on the waist with the fist-palm up. Eyes look at the left fist.（Figure 114）

Key point: the whole action shall be coherent and quick, snap the shoulders to release force, and the force shall reach fist-face.

炮
拳

圖 115

36. 叉步斜形
Diagonal posture in cross stance

（1）接上勢。身體略向右轉，右腿向左腳後插步；
同時，兩拳隨身走上弧合抱於胸前，右拳在外，左拳
在裏，兩拳心均向裏。（圖 115）

（1）Follow the above posture, turn the body to the right
slightly. Move the right leg to left foot into back cross stance. At
the same time, the two fists draw upper curve with the body,
then hold them together before the chest. Keep the right fist
outside and the left one inside, with both fist-palms inward.
（Figure 115）

炮拳套路動作圖解

圖 116

(2) 上動不停。左拳向左後方撐拳，右拳向前撐拳，兩臂微屈，拳眼相對，兩拳心均向下，高與肩平；目視前方。（圖116）

(2) Keep the above action, support the left fist left backward, and support the right fist forward. Bend the two arms slightly with the fist—holes opposite and fist—palms down at the shoulders height. Eyes look forward.（Figure 116）

炮
拳

圖 117

37. 回身一捶 Turn round and punch

（1）接上勢。身體右轉 90°，左腳尖內扣，重心移至右腿成半馬步；同時，左拳收抱於腰間，拳心向上；右拳隨身向外畫弧，再向裏擺壓於胸前，拳心向下，拳眼向裏；目視右拳。（圖 117）

（1）Follow the above posture, turn the body 90° to the right. Turn the left tiptoe inward, and transfer the barycenter to the right leg into half horse stance. At the same time, draw back and hold the left fist on the waist with the fist–palm up; the right fist draws a curve outward with the body, then swing and press it inward before the chest, with the fist–palm down and fist–hole inward. Eyes look at the right fist.（Figure 117）

圖 118

(2) 上動不停。重心前移至左腿成左弓步；同時，右拳抱於腰間，拳心向上；左拳向前平沖，拳心向下，高與肩平；目視左拳。（圖 118）

(2) Keep the above action, transfer the barycenter forward to the left leg to form left bow stance. At the same time, hold the right fist on the waist with the fist-palm up; the left fist strikes forward horizontally with the fist-palm down at the shoulders height. Eyes look at the left fist.〔Figure 118〕

炮
拳

圖 119

第四段　Section　Four

38. 轉身雙絕雙分腿　Double punches and double separations with body turn

(1)接上勢。右轉身 180°，重心前移成右弓步；同時，兩拳變掌，兩掌一起從胸前向右膝前方探出，掌心向下，掌指向前；目視兩掌。（圖 119）

炮
拳
套
路
動
作
圖
解

(1) Follow the above posture, turn the body 180° to the right. Transfer the barycenter forward into right bow stance. At the same time, change two fists into palms, stretch both palms together from the front of the chest to front of the right knee, with palm down and fingers up. Eyes look at two palms. (Figure 119)

炮
拳

圖 120

　　(2) 上動不停。重心後移，右膝提起，左腿獨立；
同時，兩掌抓握變拳收抱於腰間，拳心均向上；目視
前方。（圖120）

　　(2) Keep the above action, transfer the barycenter backward,
lift the right knee and stand on the left leg. At the same time,
two palms clench into fists, then draw back and hold them on the
waist with fist–palms up. Eyes look forward. 〔Figure 120〕

圖 121

（3）上動不停。右腳向前跨一步，左腳隨即跟步，重心落於兩腿間；同時，兩拳向前平沖，兩拳眼相對，拳心均向下，高與肩平；目視前方。（圖 121 ）

(3) Keep the above action, the right foot takes a stride forward, then the left foot follows up with the barycenter falling between two legs. At the same time, punch two fists forward horizontally with fist-holes opposite and fist-palms down at the shoulders height. Eyes look forward. (Figure 121)

炮
拳

圖 122

　(4) 上動不停。右腳向前上一小步，左腳向前併步，身體下蹲成蹲步；同時，兩拳從上向下劈拳，落於兩腿外側，兩拳眼均向裏，拳面均向下；目視前下方。（圖 122）

　　要點：同第 19 式。

　(4) Keep the above action, the right foot steps a small step forward, and move the left foot forward to bring feet together, the body squats into squatting stance. At the same time, two fists hack from upward to downward and fall at the outer sides of two legs, with fist-holes inward and fist-plane down. Eyes look down-ward ahead.〔 Figure 122 〕

　　Key point: the same as that of Posture 19.

圖 123

39. 起身雙風貫耳 Rise body to strike the opponent's ears with both fists

(1) 接上勢。重心微上提；同時，兩拳分別從身體兩側向上抬起，拳心均向下，拳眼均向前，高與肩平；目視前方。（圖 123）

(1) Follow the above posture, raise the barycenter slightly. At the same time, lift two fists from both sides of the body respectively with fist-palms down and fist-holes forward at the shoulders level. Eyes look forward.（Figure 123）

圖 124

　　(2) 上動不停。兩腳以腳跟為軸，隨身體起立左轉90°，成併步；同時，兩臂屈肘，兩拳內旋，從身兩側向裏合擊，兩拳輪相對，拳心均向裏，高與肩平；目視前方。（圖 124、圖124 附圖）

　　要點：同第 20 式。

圖 124 附圖

(2) Keep the above action, the body stands up and turn to the left by 90° with both heels as the pivots, to bring the feet together. At the same time, bend the elbows, whirl two fists inward and close inward from both sides of the body with two fist-wheels opposite and fist-palms inward at shoulder height. Eyes look forward. (Figure 124, Attached figure 124)

Key point: the same as that of Posture 20.

圖 125

40. 轉身躍步單叉
Turn body and jump into single split

(1) 接上勢。身體略左轉，左腳向左上步，右腳跟離地；左拳變掌，向下、向前上方畫掌，掌心向下；右拳變掌，向外、向下畫掌，再走下弧，向上與左掌擊響，右掌背貼於左掌心，高與頭頂平；目視兩掌。（圖 125）

炮
拳
套
路
動
作
圖
解

(1) Follow the above posture, the body turns to the left slightly, the left foot steps leftward, and the right heel leaves the ground. Change the left fist into palm, then swing the palm downward and upward ahead, with the palm down; change the right fist into palm, swing the palm outward and downward, then swing the right palm in lower curve and clap upward with the left palm. The right palm back sticks to the left palm at the head top level. Eyes look at two palms. (Figure 125)

炮拳

圖126

　　(2) 上動不停。左腳蹬地，兩腿騰空跳起；同時，右掌變拳收抱於腰間，拳心向上；左掌向右、向下畫弧，掌心向下落於胸前，掌心向右，掌指向上；目視左方。（圖126、圖126附圖）

炮
拳
套
路
動
作
圖
解

圖 126 附圖

(2) Keep the above action, the left foot presses against the ground, then two legs jump up in the air. At the same time, change the right palm into fist, draw back and hold the right fist on the waist with fist–palm up. The left palm draws a curve rightward and downward, then falls before the chest with the palm down, keep the palm rightward and fingers up. Eyes look leftward. (Figure 126, Attached figure 126)

炮
拳

圖 127

（3）上動不停。右腳落地，左腳隨即向左鏟出，身
體下蹲成左仆步；同時，左掌從胸前沿左腿向左切
掌，掌心向下，掌緣向左；目視左掌。（圖 127）

要點：雙腳跳步要輕靈快捷，仆步和切掌同時完
成。

(3) Keep the above action, the right foot lands to the ground,
then the left foot shovels leftward, the body squats into left
crouch stance. At the same time, the left palm cuts leftward from
the front of the chest along the left leg, with the palm down and
palm edge leftward. Eyes look at the left palm.〔Figure 127〕

Key points: two feet jumping shall be light and prompt; the
crouch stance and palm cutting shall be completed simultaneously.

圖 128 圖

41. 起身沖天炮　Sky cannon with body rise

（1）接上勢。身體起立，重心前移成左高弓步；同時，左掌向裏摟手變拳，拳心向下，左臂屈肘高與肩平；目視前方。（圖128）

(1) Follow the above posture, the body stands up, transfer the barycenter forward into left high bow stance. At the same time, grab the left palm inward and change it into fist with fist-palm down, bend the left elbow at the shoulders level. Eyes look forward.（Figure 128）

炮

拳

圖 129

（2）上動不停。重心前移，右膝提起成左獨立勢；
同時，左拳屈臂收於胸前，拳心向裏，拳眼向上；右
拳經左前臂內側向上沖拳，拳心向裏，拳面向上；左
拳背貼於右肘下；目視右拳。（圖 129）

　　要點：左腿獨立重心穩固，右沖拳要抖肩發力，
然後自然彈回，力達拳面。

炮
拳
套
路
動
作
圖
解

(2) Keep the above action, transfer the barycenter forward, lift the right knee into left stance on one leg. At the same time, bend left arm and draw back the left fist before the chest with fist-palm inward and fist-hole up, the right fist strikes upward through the inner side of the left forearm, with fist-palm inward and fist-plane up. The left fist back sticks to the bottom of the right elbow. Eyes look at the right fist. (Figure 129)

Key points: the barycenter shall be firm for stance on the left leg, snap the shoulders to apply force for the right fist striking with natural rebound, and the force shall reach the fist-plane.

圖 130

42. 束身下劈腿　Shrink body and hack down

　（1）接上勢。身體微向右轉，右腳向右後方落步，重心落於兩腿間；目視前方。（圖 130、圖 130 附圖）

炮拳套路動作圖解

圖 130 附圖

(1) Follow the above posture, turn the body to the right slightly. The right foot lands right backward. The barycenter falls between two legs. Eyes look forward.（Figure 130, Attached figure 130）

圖 131

　　⑵上動不停。身體右轉 90°，左腳收回，腳尖點地，身體下蹲成丁步；同時，兩拳變為鉗子手，右手下劈落於右小腿外側，掌指向下，虎口向前；左手護於左肩前，虎口向外，掌指向上；目視右手。（圖131、圖 131 附圖）

炮
拳
套
路
動
作
圖
解

圖 131 附圖

(2) Keep the above action, turn the body 90° to the right.
Draw back the left foot with the tiptoe on the ground, squat the
body into T−stance. At the same time, change two fists into
pincers hands, hack the right hand downward, then the right hand
falls at the outer side of the right lower leg, with fingers
downward and tiger′s mouth forward. The left hand guards
before the left shoulder with tiger′s mouth outward, and fingers
up. Eyes look at the right hand. 〔Figure 131, Attached figure
131〕

炮拳

圖 132

43. 起身五指朝鳳

Fingers toward the phoenix with body rise

接上勢。身體起立，左腿提膝，右腿獨立；同時，右手經胸前屈肘上托，手心向後、掌指向上護於右肩前；左手變鉤手擺至身後，鉤尖向上；目視左方。（圖 132、圖 132 附圖）

炮拳套路動作圖解

圖 132 附圖

Follow the above posture, the body stands up, lift the left knee and stand on the right leg. At the same time, bend the right elbow to lift the right hand through the front of chest with palm backward and fingers upward, guarding before the right shoulder. Chang the left hand into hook hand and swing it to the back of the body, with hook-tip up. Eyes look leftward. ﹝Figure 132, Attached figure 132﹞

炮
拳

圖 133

44. 轉身雲頂七星

Turn body and cloud top into seven stars

（1）接上勢。左腳向左側落地；同時，左鉤手變掌，由外向裏畫弧，雲托於頭頂上方；右掌向外、向上雲托，置於頭右側方，高與頭頂平，兩掌心均向上，掌指均向右；目視右掌。（圖 133）

（1）Follow the above posture, the left foot falls to the ground at the left side. At the same time, change the left hook hand into palm and draw a curve from inward to outward, cloud the hand above the head top; cloud the right palm outward and upward, then place it above the right side of the head at the head top level. With two palms up and all the fingers rightward. Eyes look at the right palm.（Figure 133）

圖 134

(2) 上動不停。身體右轉 180°，右腳提起隨轉身向右橫開一步；同時，右掌向後、向左雲托於頭頂；左掌向後、向外雲托於頭左側方，高與頭頂平，兩掌心均向上，掌指均向左；目視左掌。（圖 134）

(2) Keep the above action, turn the body to the right by 180°, lift the right foot and stride a step rightward with the body turn. At the same time, the right palm lifts above the head top backward and leftward; the left palm lifts backward and outward to the left side of the head at the head top level. With two palms up and all the fingers leftward. Eyes look at the left palm. (Figure 134)

炮

拳

圖 135

(3) 上動不停。右腳尖外擺，身體右轉 90°，左腳跟離地；同時，兩掌變拳收抱於腰間，拳心向上；目視前方。（圖135）

(3) Keep the above action, turn the right tiptoe out-ward and the body 90° to the right. The left heel leaves the ground, at the same time, change two palms into fists, then draw back and hold them on the waist, with fist-palms up. Eyes look forward. （Figure 135）

圖 136

　(4) 上動不停。左腳向前上步成丁步；同時，右拳向前平沖，拳心向下，拳眼向左，高與肩平；左臂屈肘前撐，拳面抵於右肘內側，拳心向下；目視右拳。（圖 136）

　要點：同第 6 式。

　(4) Keep the above action, the left foot steps forward into T-stance. At the same time, the right fist strikes for-ward horizontally, with fist-palm down and fist-hole leftward at the shoulders height; bend the left elbow to support forward, with the fist-plane propped to the inner side of the right elbow and fist-palm down. Eyes look at the right fist. (Figure 136)

　Key point: same as form 6.

圖 137

45. 馬步單鞭　Single whip in horse stance

（1）接上勢。身體左轉 90°，左腳向左橫跨一步成馬步；同時，兩拳外旋，屈肘合於胸前併齊，拳心向裏，高與肩平；目視兩拳。（圖 137）

（1）Follow the above posture, turn the body 90° to left, the left foot strides a step leftward into horse stance. At the same time, whirl two fists outward and bend the elbows to close together before the chest, with fist–palm inward at the shoulders height. Eyes look at two fists.（Figure 137）

炮拳套路動作圖解

圖 138

(2) 上動不停。兩拳分別向身體兩側平沖，拳心均向下，拳眼均向前，高與肩平；目視左拳。（圖 138）

要點：同第 7 式。

(2) Keep the above action, two fists horizontally strike to both sides of the body respectively, with fist—palms down and fist—holes forward at the shoulders height. Eyes look at the left fist.（Figure 138）

Key point: the same as that of Posture 7.

圖 139

46. 五花坐山　Swing arms with horse stance

（1）接上勢。身體起立，重心移至左腿，同時，收右腳，向身體右側震腳落地；目視右方。（圖 139）

(1) Follow the above posture, stand up, and transfer the barycenter to the left leg. At the same time, draw back the right foot to right side of the body and stamp it to the ground. Eyes look rightward.〔Figure 139〕

圖 140

(2) 上動不停。身體左轉 90°，隨即左腳提起向前上一步；同時，左拳向上、向裏畫弧，屈肘落於胸前，拳眼向裏，拳心向下；右臂隨身走下弧，向前、向上擺拳，置於左膝上方，拳眼向上；目視右拳。（圖 140）

(2) Keep the above action, turn the body 90° to the left, then lift the left foot and takes a step forward. At the same time, the left fist draws a curve upward and inward and falls before the chest with the elbow bent, the fist–hole inward and the fist–palm down; the right arm draws lower curve with the body to swing forward and upward, then place it above the left knee, with fist–hole up. Eyes look at the right fist. (Figure 140)

炮

拳

圖 141

(3) 上動不停。身體右轉 90°成馬步；同時，左拳經胸前向下栽拳，拳面頂於左膝蓋上，拳心向後；右拳向上架於頭部右上方，拳心向前，拳眼向下，發「威」聲；目視左方。（圖 141）

要點：震腳有力，發聲響亮、渾厚。

(3) Keep the above action, turn the body to the right by 90° into horse stance. At the same time, the left fist punches downward through the front of the chest, the fist-plane props the left knee with fist-palm backward; the right fist parries upward above the right part of the head with fist-palm forward and fist-hole down. Send " Vee" sound. Eyes look leftward. (Figure 141)

Key point: stamp the feet forcefully; send sound loudly and thickly.

炮拳套路動作圖解

圖 142

47. 收勢　Closing form

⑴上動不停。身體起立，收左腳向右成併步；同時，兩掌變拳抱於腰間；目視前方。（圖 142）

⑴ Keep the above action, stand up, and withdraw and move the left foot to the right side to bring feet together. At the same time, change two palms into fists and hold them on the waist. Eyes look forward.（Figure 142）

圖 143

（2）上動不停，兩拳同時自然下垂至身體兩側；目視前方。（圖 143）

要點：挺胸收腹，平心靜氣，體態自然，精神內斂。

(2) Keep the above action, two fists drop naturally to both sides of the body simultaneously. Eyes look forward.〔 Figure 143 〕

Key points: lift the chest and draw in the abdomen, be calm in natural posture, and collect the vital energy inward.

全套動作演示圖
Demonstration of All the Action

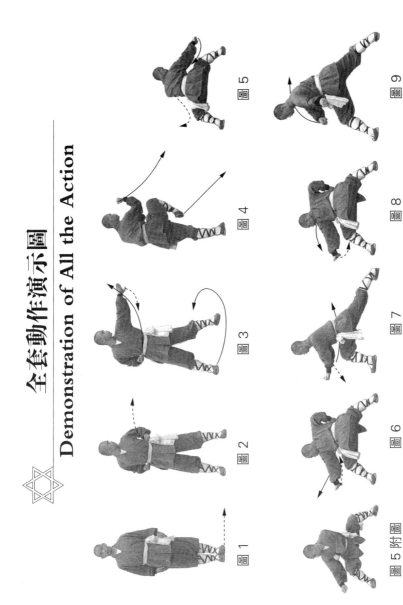

圖1　圖2　圖3　圖4　圖5

圖5附圖　圖6　圖7　圖8　圖9

羅漢拳

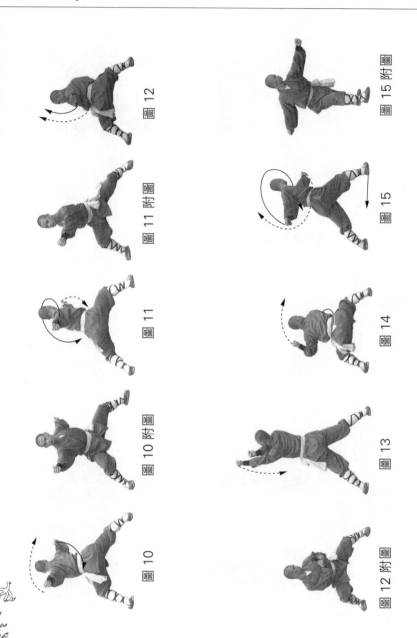

圖 12

圖 11 附圖

圖 11

圖 10 附圖

圖 10

圖 15 附圖

圖 15

圖 14

圖 13

圖 12 附圖

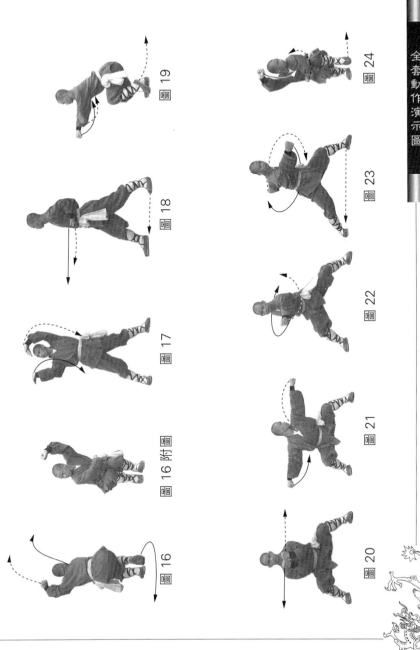

全套動作演示圖

羅漢拳

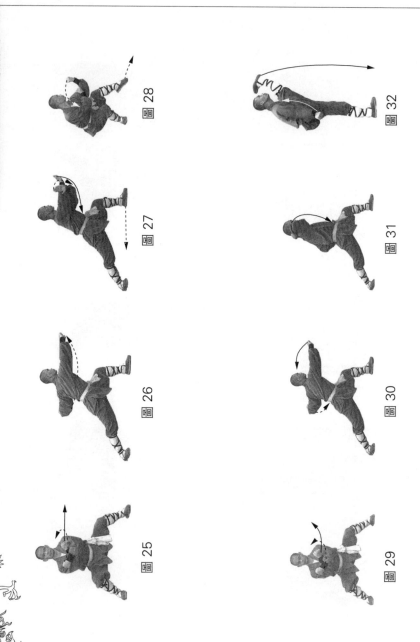

圖 28

圖 32

圖 27

圖 31

圖 26

圖 30

圖 25

圖 29

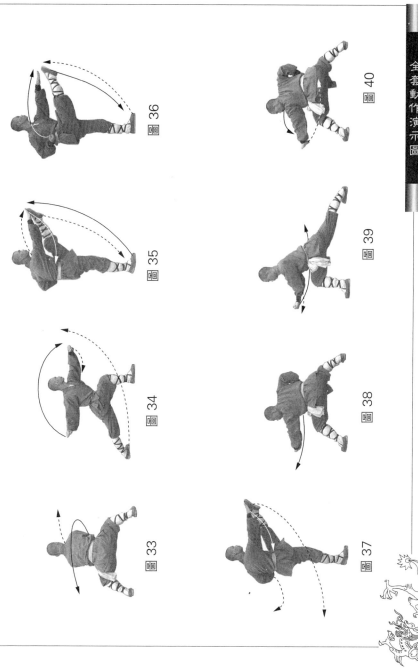

全套動作演示圖

圖 40

圖 39

圖 38

圖 37

圖 36

圖 35

圖 34

圖 33

羅漢拳

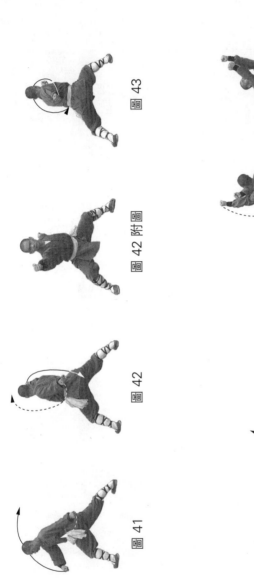

圖 41

圖 42

圖 42 附圖

圖 43

圖 43 附圖

圖 44

圖 44 附圖

圖 45

圖 45 附圖

全套動作演示圖

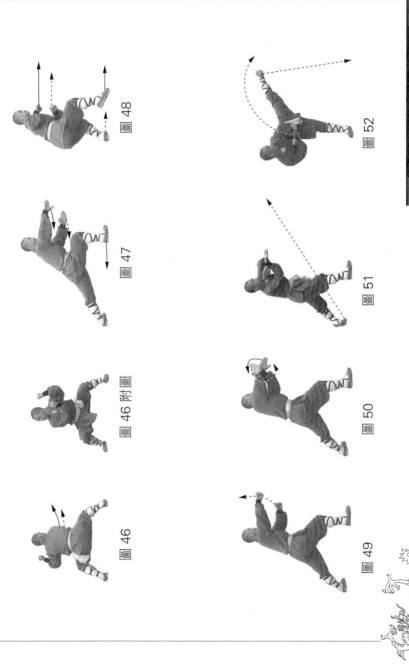

圖 48

圖 47

圖 46 附圖

圖 46

圖 52

圖 51

圖 50

圖 49

羅漢拳

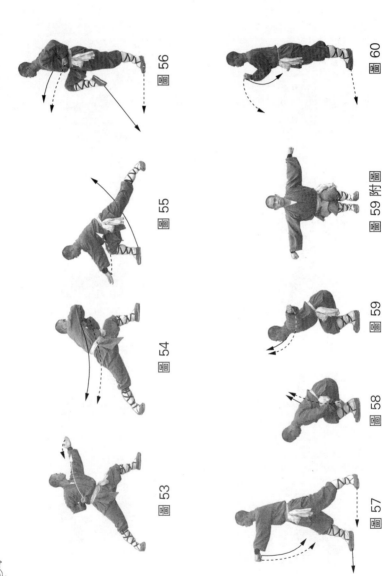

圖 56

圖 55

圖 54

圖 53

圖 60

圖 59 附圖

圖 59

圖 58

圖 57

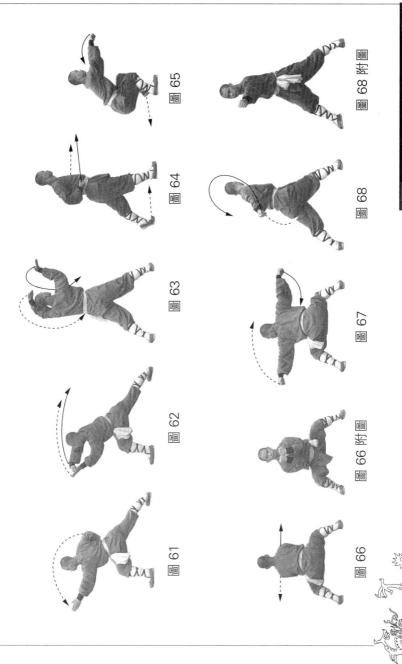

圖 65　圖 64　圖 63　圖 62　圖 61

圖 68 附圖　圖 68　圖 67　圖 66 附圖　圖 66

全套動作演示圖

羅漢拳

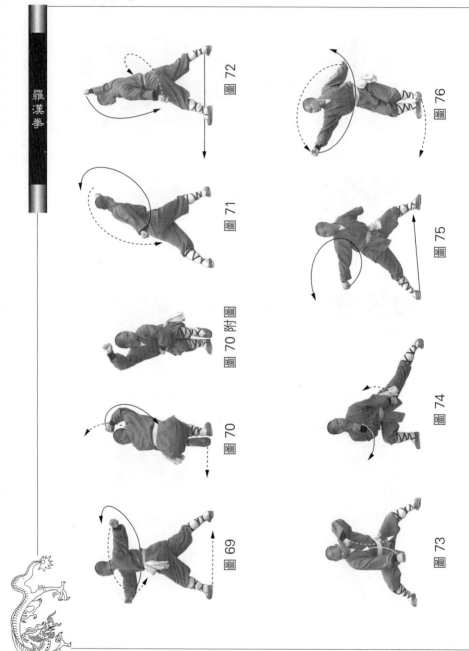

圖 72

圖 71

圖 70 附圖

圖 70

圖 69

圖 76

圖 75

圖 74

圖 73

全套動作演示圖

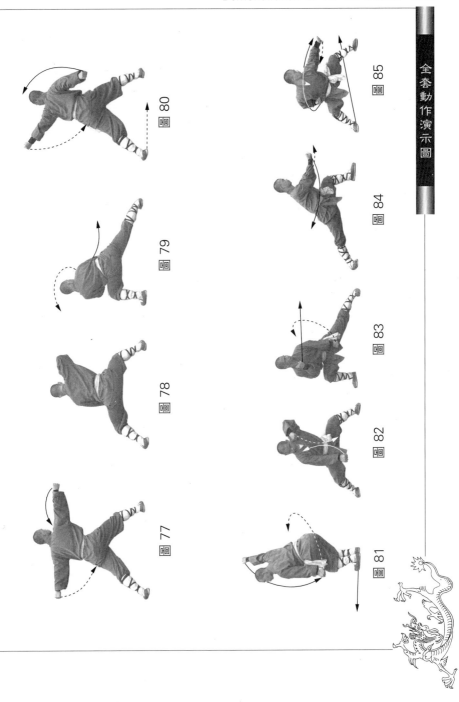

圖 77

圖 78

圖 79

圖 80

圖 81

圖 82

圖 83

圖 84

圖 85

羅漢拳

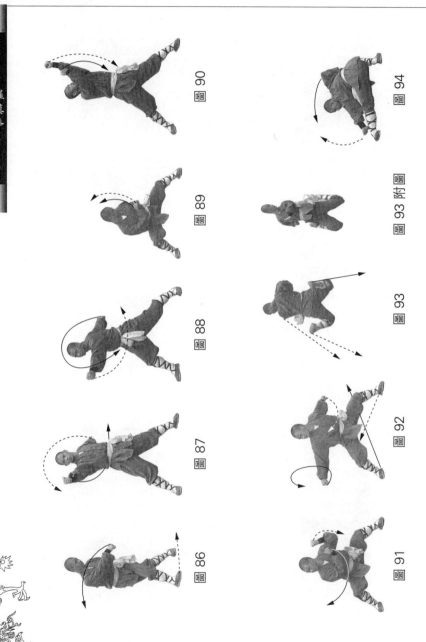

圖 90

圖 89

圖 88

圖 87

圖 86

圖 94

圖 93 附圖

圖 93

圖 92

圖 91

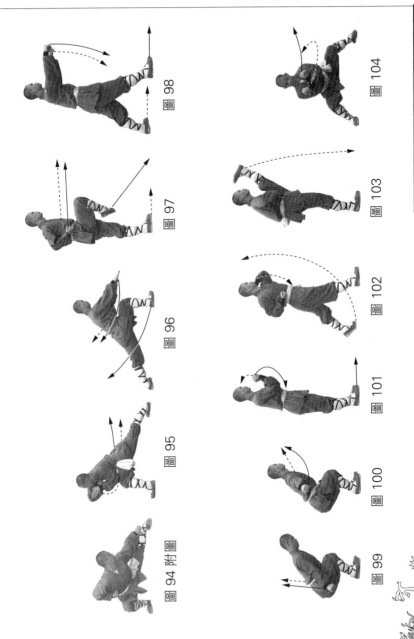

全套動作演示圖

圖 98

圖 97

圖 96

圖 95

圖 94 附圖

圖 104

圖 103

圖 102

圖 101

圖 100

圖 99

羅漢拳

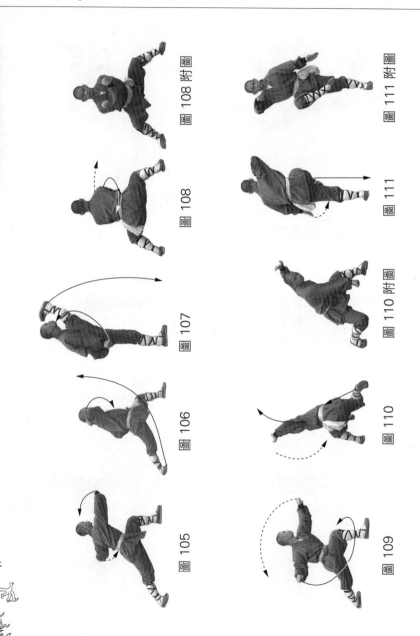

圖 108 附圖　　圖 108

圖 111 附圖　　圖 111

圖 107　　圖 106　　圖 105

圖 110 附圖　　圖 110　　圖 109

全套動作演示圖

圖 114

圖 113

圖 112 附圖

圖 112

圖 118

圖 117

圖 116

圖 115

羅漢拳

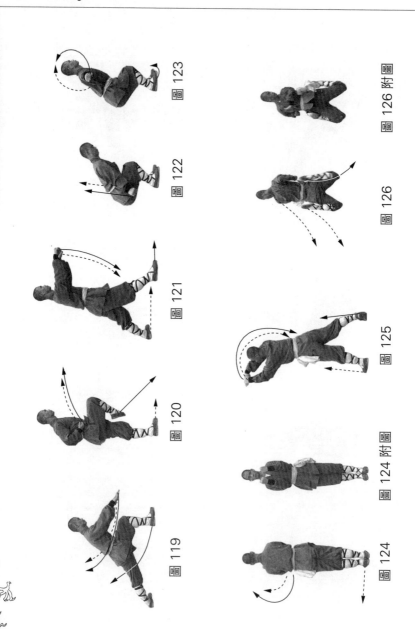

圖 123　圖 122　圖 121　圖 120　圖 119

圖 126 附圖　圖 126　圖 125　圖 124 附圖　圖 124

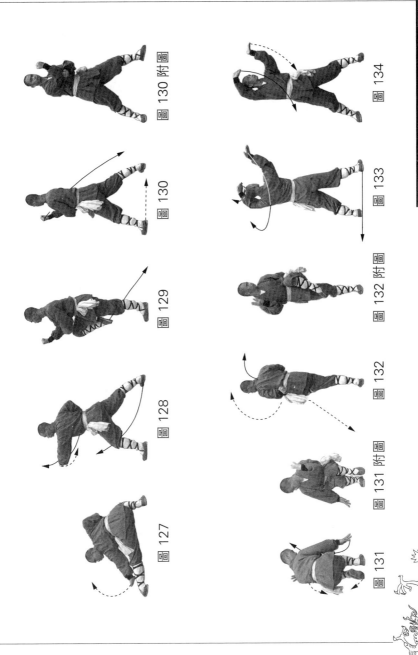

全套動作演示圖

圖 130 附圖

圖 130

圖 129

圖 128

圖 127

圖 134

圖 133

圖 132 附圖

圖 132

圖 131 附圖

圖 131

羅漢拳

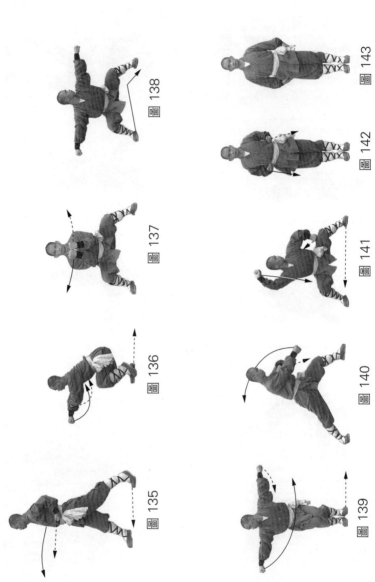

圖 138

圖 143

圖 142

圖 137

圖 141

圖 136

圖 140

圖 135

圖 139

導引養生功

輕鬆學武術

國家圖書館出版品預行編目資料

炮　拳 = Cannon Boxing/ 耿　軍　著
　　　——初版，——臺北市，大展，2008〔民 97.03〕
　　　面；21 公分，——（少林傳統功夫漢英對照系列；10）
　　　ISBN　978 – 957 – 468 – 598 – 1（平裝）

1. 少林拳　2. 中國
528.97　　　　　　　　　　　　　　　　　　97000411

炮　拳

ISBN 978 – 957 – 468 – 598 – 1

著　　者/耿　　軍
責任編輯/張　建　林
發 行 人/蔡　森　明
出 版 者/大展出版社有限公司
社　　址/台北市北投區（石牌）致遠一路 2 段 12 巷 1 號
電　　話/（02）28236031・28236033・28233123
傳　　眞/（02）28272069
郵政劃撥/01669551
網　　址/ www.dah-jaan.com.tw
E - mail / service@dah-jaan.com.tw
登 記 證/局版臺業字第 2171 號
承 印 者/傳興印刷有限公司
裝　　訂/建鑫裝訂有限公司
排 版 者/弘益電腦排版有限公司
授 權 者/北京人民體育出版社
初版 1 刷/2008 年（民 97 年）3 月

定　　價/220 元

推理文學經典巨著，中文版正式授權

名偵探明智小五郎與怪盜的挑戰與鬥智

名偵探柯南、金田一都讚嘆不已

日本推理小說鼻祖─江戶川亂步

1894年10月21日出生於日本三重縣名張〈現在的名張市〉。本名平井太郎。
就讀於早稻田大學時就曾經閱讀許多英、美的推理小說。
畢業之後曾經任職於貿易公司，也曾經擔任舊書商、新聞記者等各種工作。
1923年4月，在『新青年』中發表「二錢銅幣」。
筆名江戶川亂步是根據推理小說的始祖艾德嘉・亞藍波而取的。
後來致力於創作許多推理小說。
1936年配合「少年俱樂部」的要求所寫的『怪盜二十面相』極受人歡迎，
陸續發表『少年偵探團』、『妖怪博士』共26集……等
適合少年、少女閱讀的作品。

1～3集 定價300元 試閱特價189元